Functional
Lessons
in
Singing

3rd Edition

IVAN TRUSLER
Bowling Green State University

WALTER EHRET

Prentice-Hall, Inc.
Englewood Cliffs, N.J. 07632

Library of Congress Cataloging-in-Publication Data

Trusler, Ivan.
  Functional lessons in singing

  Contains 40 songs.
  Bibliography: p.
  1. Singing—Diction. I. Ehret, Walter. II. Title.
MT872.T7 1987   784.9′32   86-9493
ISBN 0-13-331778-1

Editorial/production supervision and interior design: Mark Stevens
Manufacturing buyer: Ray Keating

Printed in the United States of America
10 9 8 7 6 5

ISBN 0-13-331778-1 01

Prentice-Hall International (UK) Limited, *London*
Prentice-Hall of Australia Pty. Limited, *Sydney*
Prentice-Hall Canada, Inc., *Toronto*
Prentice-Hall Hispanoamericana, S.A., *Mexico*
Prentice-Hall of India Private Limited, *New Delhi*
Prentice-Hall of Japan, Inc., *Tokyo*
Prentice-Hall of Southeast Asia Pte. Ltd., *Singapore*
Editora Prentice-Hall do Brasil, Ltda., *Rio de Janeiro*
Whitehall Books Limited, *Wellington, New Zealand*

Contents

Preface

Purpose and Content

This book presents a functional series of lessons through which students may develop specific vocal and musical abilities based on the sounds of the English language.

After the first lesson, which seeks to establish proper breathing and breath control, each chapter takes up a different vowel, diphthong, or consonant. Words and sentences with the particular sound are read aloud, then sung. A study section includes a description of the vowel, diphthong, or consonant, and its proper execution. Common faults and how to correct them are discussed, along with general principles of singing. Each lesson includes an art song with a training text constructed on the sound being studied, as well as the original text.

Special Features

All material is directly related to specific problems and goals. For example, a "Song Interpretation and Musicianship" section precedes *and is based on* the art song in each lesson. Musical terms and stylistic and interpretive principles are learned *as they appear in each song.*

All English vowels, diphthongs, and consonants are discussed. The phonetic symbols from *Webster's New World Dictionary*, the *American Heritage Dictionary*, and the International Phonetic Alphabet are employed.

In addition to the song in each lesson, there are twenty-two more songs at the back, making forty in all, some of which were composed specifically for this book.

A graded and categorized list of selected song titles appears at the end of the book, with a list of publishers and their addresses.

Suggested Uses

This book is designed for use in the high school, college, conservatory, or church. It is intended primarily as a "class voice" book, but can be equally effective in the private studio. It would be ideal as a training manual for mixed, treble, or male choirs. It can also serve as a reference text.

The authors have based this book on many years of experience as musicians and educators. From its wide acceptance throughout the United States, the verdict seems apparent—it works! The present edition seeks to make it work even better. We have given the book a general editing overhaul. A guide to pronunciation symbols and phonetics has been added. Several songs have been removed, and a larger number of fresh ones has been added. Major changes were made in two chapters, and a new chapter on diphthongs was added. The categorized and graded list of songs and the list of collections have been expanded and updated.

Ivan Trusler
Walter Ehret

GUIDE TO SYMBOLS
USED FOR PRONUNCIATION

Sample words	Phonetic spellings used in this edition	Webster's New World Dictionary	American Heritage Dictionary	International Phonetic Alphabet
Vowels				
mat, pat, can	ĂH	a	ă	æ
farm, large, charge	AH	ä	ä	ɑ
pet, met, let	EH	e	ĕ	ɛ
bee, see, we	EE	ē	ē	i
pit, bit, miss	IH	i	ĭ	ɪ
omit, obey, occur	OH	no symbol*	no symbol*	o
paw, cause, law	AW	ô	ô	ɔ
book, crook, took	OŎ	oo	o͝o	ʊ
moon, lose, soon	OO	o͞o	o͞o	u
cut, but, luck	UH	u	ŭ	ʌ
sofa, ocean, treasure	(weak vowel)	ə	ə	ə
bird, learn, word	(umlaut vowel)	ʉ	û	ɜ
Diphthongs				
may, pay, say	EH͡IH	ā	ā	ɛɪ
my, I, pie	AH͡IH	ī	ī	aɪ
Oh, no, cold	OH͡OŎ	ō	ō	oʊ
noise, boy, Roy	AW͡IH	oi	oi	ɔɪ
out, cloud, how	AH͡UH	ou	ou	aʊ
cute, few, view	IH͡OO	yo͞o	yo͞o	ɪu
fair, hair, rare	(fair)	er	âr	ɛə
fear, here, beer	(fear)	ir	îr	ɪə
four, more, sore	(four)	ôr	r	ɔə

Webster's New World Dictionary and the *American Heritage Dictionary* treat unstressed o as a diphthong (ō).

Consonants

	Webster's New World Dictionary	American Heritage Dictionary	International Phonetic Alphabet
bib, Bob, bad	b	b	b
church, chant, chill	ch	ch	tʃ
dead, dad, dude	d	d	d
fife, feel, feed	f	f	f
gag, good, girl	g	g	g
hat, hoe, had	h	h	h
which, what, when	hw	hw	hw
judge, just, jest	j	j	dʒ
kick, come, king	K	K	K
Lil, leap, long	l	l	l
mum, mean, mom	m	m	m
no, noon, night	n	n	n
thing, ring, sing	ŋ	ng	ŋ
pop, pend, past	p	p	p
roar, rip, rent	r	r	r
sis, song, sing	s	s	s
ship, shoe, she	sh	sh	ʃ
tight, tent, toe	t	t	t
thin, thing, thank	th	th	ө
this, that, those	th	th	ð
valve, vase, view	v	v	v
with, want, was	w	w	w
yes, yawn, use	y	y	j
zest, zebra, zero	z	z	z

LESSON 1

Breathing and Breath Control

BREATHING EXERCISES

Good posture is the foundation of controlled breathing, and controlled breathing is the foundation of singing.

1. From a sitting position, lean forward and place your forearms on your knees. Take a slow, deep, noiseless breath through the mouth. Expand the waistline entirely, but do not raise the shoulders, then exhale. The muscles in action will be the abdominal (stomach), dorsal (back), and costal (rib) muscles. (See Figure 1–8.)

2. Sit up with your back straight and chest high. Repeat exercise 1 in this position.

3. Inhale deeply, then exhale slowly with a steady hissing sound while counting to 24. (The abdominal, dorsal, and costal muscles should continue to be involved.)

4. Stand up with your back straight, chest high, feet apart, one foot slightly in front of the other, with weight on the forward foot. Place your hands on your hips.

    Exhale, contracting (pulling in) the abdominal, dorsal, and costal muscles.

    Inhale deeply, allowing the abdominal, dorsal, and costal muscles to expand. You should have a feeling of lift from the abdomen upward, but do not raise your shoulders.

    Exhale very slowly, with a hissing sound.

BREATH CONTROL EXERCISES

The starting pitch of each exercise throughout the book should be comfortable for most voices, but may be varied at the discretion of the teacher. This and all other exercises are to be repeated, transposing up and down by half-steps, throughout the entire vocal range.

Hum these exercises on "mmm." Continue breathing as instructed.

1. Very slowly.

2. Very slowly.

3. Slowly; be sure the second pitch (major third) is high enough.

4. Very slowly; sing with one breath.

5. Moderately; sing with one breath.

6. Very slowly.[1]

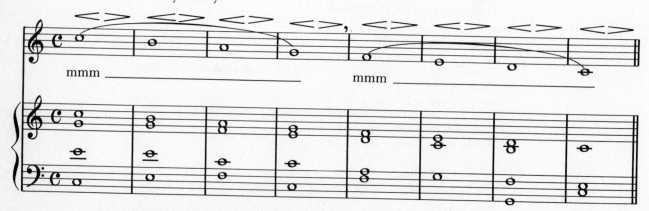

---

1. This descending scale is harmonized here for use throughout the book. The piano part can also be sung, in two, three, or four parts.

7. Moderately; sing with one breath.

mmm

STUDY

Correct breathing and breath control are largely dependent upon the action of the diaphragm and the rib cage. The diaphragm is a muscle wall situated between the stomach and the lungs. At rest, the diaphragm forms two semicircular domes upon which the bases of the lungs rest. (See Figure 1–9.) During respiration (breathing), the diaphragm acts as follows:

1. *Inhalation* (Figure 1–2). As air is inhaled, the centers of the domes flatten, creating a space between the diaphragm and the lungs. Atmospheric pressure outside the body forces air through the respiratory tract into the area of decreased air pressure at the bottom of the lungs. The lungs expand to fill this space. As the rib cage expands, a larger cavity is formed, which helps to force air into the lungs.
2. *Exhalation.* As air is exhaled, the two domes return to their original positions, giving additional power to the expulsion of the breath. This action plays an important role in singing, providing energy and firm support at all dynamic levels throughout the range.

To feel the action of the diaphragm, place the tips of the fingers below the breastbone and puff as though blowing out a candle. Note that, before the puff of breath, a deep inhalation takes place. Note the movement of the lower ribs and abdominal muscles.

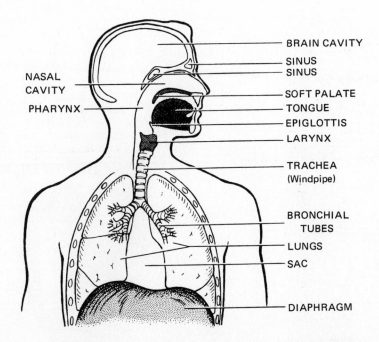

FIGURE 1–1

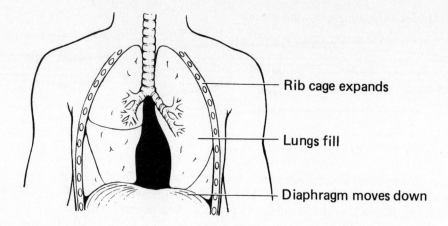

— Rib cage expands

— Lungs fill

— Diaphragm moves down

FIGURE 1–2

Breathing:
Common Faults and Corrections

Poor posture is one of the chief causes of incorrect breathing. Good posture is essential to controlled breathing.

GENERAL RULES FOR GOOD POSTURE:
1. **Hold head comfortably erect.**
2. **Shoulders should remain down.**
3. **Carry chest high.**
4. **Keep back straight.**

Figures 1–3 and 1–4 show the two most common errors of breathing; Figures 1–5 and 1–6 show the correct method.

FIGURE 1–3
High Chest Breathing (Incorrect)

FIGURE 1–4
Lower Abdominal Breathing (Incorrect)

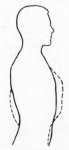

FIGURE 1–5
Diaphragmatic Breathing (Correct)

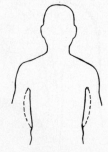

FIGURE 1–6
Costal Breathing (Correct)

Application of Breathing Principles to Singing

Deep, full breathing is prerequisite to a beautiful singing tone, and control of the breath is vital to beautiful tone. Enrico Caruso, the great Italian tenor, said that he spent his entire life working to produce a maximum of tone with a minimum of breath. Control of breath is usually dependent on three factors.

1. The *diaphragm* controls the flow of air into and out of the lungs through the trachea (windpipe). The breathing system is both voluntary and involuntary: though we can control our breathing, our bodies breathe automatically when we do not exercise conscious control. Ideally, the diaphragm is under perfect mental control, responding to the singer's slightest wish as it works in a balanced action with the costal and abdominal muscles.

2. The *vocal bands* (or *vocal cords*) resist the outgoing stream of breath from the trachea. Air passing through the vocal bands causes them to vibrate and produce tone. Figure 1–7 shows the vibration patterns of the vocal bands.

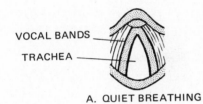

VOCAL BANDS

TRACHEA

A. QUIET BREATHING   B. BREATHY TONE   C. CLEAR TONE
(LOW PITCH)

D. CLEAR TONE
(MEDIUM PITCH)   E. CLEAR TONE
(HIGH PITCH)   F. FALSETTO

FIGURE 1–7

3. *Even breath distribution* increases and decreases in intensity as the song demands. If too much breath is used, the vocal bands do not close properly, a breathy tone results, and control of the breath may be lost. Humming is an excellent way to develop clear tone production with a minimum of breath. Most beginning students produce good tone when they hum correctly; moreover, humming gives a feeling of free resonance.

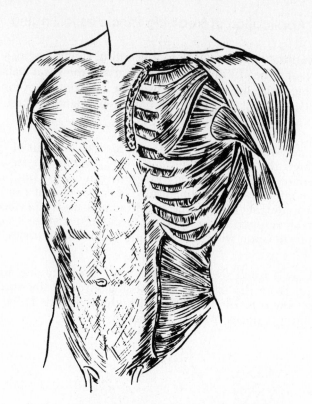

FIGURE 1–8   Stomach, Back, and Rib Muscles

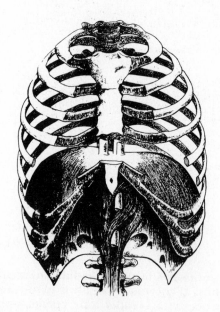

FIGURE 1–9
Diaphragm Muscle at Rest

GENERAL RULES FOR HUMMING:
1. Close lips loosely, with tongue forward and throat relaxed.
2. Do not hum below that part of the range in which the hum is clear.
3. Never hum louder than is necessary for a sense of free resonance.

The clear hum is recognized by its purity of resonance and the feeling of freedom in production. Tone vibrations are most easily felt when humming in the lower ranges. To feel these vibrations, place your hand on the top of your head, your nose, or the back of your neck. The clear hum is so resonant that its point of origin can hardly be determined. Use humming for developing a clear tone and to examine resonance on different pitches.

The singer must know not only *how* but also *where* to breathe. Examination of the text and music should reveal the correct places to take a breath. Do not depend on punctuation, especially commas; instead, find the musical phrases and breathe accordingly. For example, in the song "All Through the Night," (see page 9) do not breathe after "child"; it makes more musical sense to breathe after "thee" or "night."

Markings are often inserted in printed music to indicate where to breathe. Those most commonly used are:

apostrophe (breath marks): ,

rests: ▬ ;   ▬ ;   𝄽 ;   𝄾 ;   𝄿

slurs (phrasing marks): ⌒

GENERAL RULES FOR BREATHING:

1. **Do not breathe between the syllables of a word unless there are rests.**
2. **Do not breathe between a noun and its modifier.**
3. **Do not break up a grammatical phrase or clause.**
4. **Do not disrupt the rhythm or phrasing with inappropriate breaths.**
5. **Time for a breath should be taken from the final note of a phrase, not from the first note of a new phrase.**

SONG INTERPRETATION AND MUSICIANSHIP
Welsh Folk Song, "All Through the Night"

Hum the song and then sing it in a legato (smooth, connected) style. The rhythmic figure ♩. ♪ appears frequently; do not sing it as a triplet (𝅘𝅥𝅘𝅥𝅘𝅥) or as a double-dotted quarter note followed by a sixteenth note (♩.. ♪).

Music is constructed according to a planned design, which is called the *form.* Just as in architecture, where the terms *split-level* and *A-frame* are used to identify two different types, or forms, of house, in music the terms *strophic* and *through-composed* identify two important song forms.

Strophic songs are those in which the same music is repeated for successive stanzas of the poem, as in hymns. *Through-composed* songs use different music for each stanza of the text in order to reflect the changes in its mood and meaning, as in "Silent Noon" by Ralph Vaughan Williams (page 236 or "Columbia, the Gem of the Ocean."

The most commonly used song forms are *two-part* and *three-part form.* An example of two-part form is "America."

(Part I)
My country, 'tis of thee,
Sweet land of liberty,
Of thee I sing:

(Part II)
Land where my fathers died,
Land of the Pilgrims' pride,
From every mountainside let freedom ring!

Two- and three-part songs may also be strophic in form. ("America" is an example, since each of its stanzas is set to the same music.)

"All Through the Night" is a three-part song. Notice that measures 1–4, 5–8, and 13–16 are the same;[2] measures 9–12 are different, and therefore contrasting. If we call measures 1–4, 5–8, and 13–16 the "A" sections, and 9–12 the "B" section, we derive the following pattern:

A (A), B, A
or:
A (A) = Part I
B = Part II
A (repeated) = Part III

Most folk songs, like "All Through the Night," are in simple forms. They should be sung with simplicity and sincerity. Spend most of your practice time humming this song.

After each song throughout the book, there is a blank page of manuscript paper for use by teacher and student.

---

2.   For easy reference, each measure of each song throughout the book has been numbered.

All Through the Night

James Boulton

Welsh Folk Song

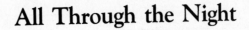

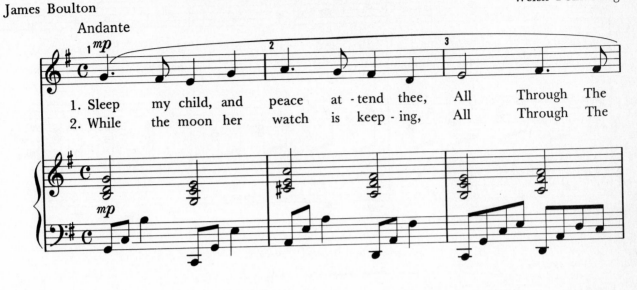

1. Sleep my child, and peace at-tend thee, All Through The Night;
2. While the moon her watch is keep-ing, All Through The Night;

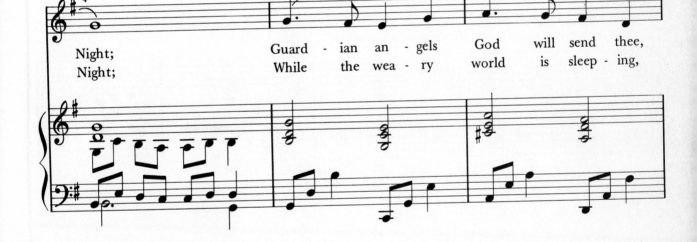

Night; Guard - ian an - gels God will send thee,
Night; While the wea - ry world is sleep - ing,

All Through The Night; Soft the drow - sy
All Through The Night; O'er thy spir - it

hours are creep - ing, Hill and vale in slum - ber steep - ing,
gen - tly steal - ing, Vis - ions of de - light re - veal - ing,

I my lov - ing vi - gil keep - ing, All Through The Night.
Breathes a pure and ho - ly feel - ing, All Through The Night.

The *EE* Vowel

[1]Webster's New World:	ē
American Heritage:	ē
International:	i

WORDS WITH THE *EE* VOWEL

Read aloud slowly:

me	sleep	yield	weave
we	each	weep	leave
key	queen	see	keep
three	please	be	beat

To warm up, first hum this exercise. Start all exercises in subsequent lessons as well by humming. *Sing all words on the first note* before moving on to the next (even though only two or three words may actually appear under each note).

1. Very slowly.

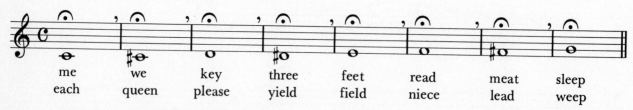

me	we	key	three	feet	read	meat	sleep
each	queen	please	yield	field	niece	lead	weep

---

1. In this and all subsequent lessons, the diacritical symbols shown within the boxes are from *Webster's New World Dictionary of the American Language,* 2nd college ed. (Collins, 1979); *The American Heritage Dictionary of the English Language* (American Heritage and Houghton Mifflin, 1969); and the International Phonetic Alphabet.

2. Very slowly.

me	be	three	eve	meat
each	cleave	yield	neat	weep

3. Very slowly; sing with one breath.

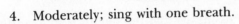

me_____	we_____	key
three_____	feet_____	read
meat_____	sleep_____	each
queen_____	please_____	yield

4. Moderately; sing with one breath.

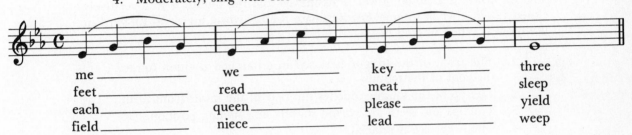

me _____	we _____	key _____	three
feet _____	read _____	meat _____	sleep
each _____	queen _____	please _____	yield
field _____	niece _____	lead _____	weep

SENTENCES WITH THE *EE* VOWEL

Sing until *EE* vowels are clearly executed.

1. Very slowly.

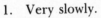

ⓐ We	see	three_____	queens.
ⓑ Re -	ceive	three_____	keys.
ⓒ Each	field	feeds_____	sheep.
ⓓ Be -	lieve	me_____	please.

2. Moderately; sing with one breath.

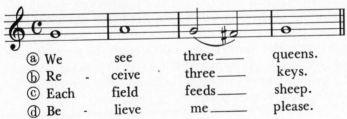

ⓐ We_____	see_____	three_____	queens.
ⓑ Re -	ceive_____	three_____	keys.
ⓒ Each_____	field_____	feeds_____	sheep.
ⓓ Be -	lieve_____	me_____	please.

3. Very slowly.

ⓐ We	see	three	queens.	ⓑ Re -	ceive	three	keys.
ⓒ Each	field	feeds	sheep.	ⓓ Be -	lieve	me	please.

4. Moderately; sing with one breath.

ⓐ We_____   see   three___   queens._____
ⓑ Re   ceive   three___   keys._____
ⓒ Each_____   field   feeds___   sheep._____
ⓓ Be   lieve   me___   please._____

STUDY

The *EE* (ē) Vowel:[2]
Description and Execution

The *EE* vowel is a closed vowel. This means that the mouth is in a relatively closed position when singing *EE*. Resonate the *EE* vowel high and forward in the mouth. When singing *EE*:

1. The front of the tongue is raised in an arched position toward the roof of the mouth.
2. The tip of the tongue touches the rear of the lower front teeth.
3. The lips and teeth are parted slightly in a smiling position.
4. The lower jaw is relaxed.

Use a hand mirror to check these and future positions as you practice.

The *EE* (i) Vowel:
Common Faults and Corrections

Differentiate between *EE* and *IH* (the vowel sound in *it*[3]); otherwise diction will not be clear and the meaning of the text will be obscured (for example, *leave* becomes *live*, *steal* becomes *still*). Form the *EE* vowel with the mouth relatively closed, resonating the vowel at the hard palate and through the nose. Do not allow the tone to sound pinched. Keep the jaw and lips free of tension. "Think" the *EE* sound. Avoid a grinning smile, which will cause undue tension in the lips and result in a lowered, too-relaxed palate and a nasal tone.

General Principles of Singing

Certain vowels are called *primary* or *fundamental;* others are called *secondary* or *subordinate* because they are considered modifications of fundamental sounds. *EE* is a fundamental vowel.[4]

The male voice must *cover* all vowels when singing full voice on high notes. To cover is to sing with a high degree of resonance concentrated at the hard palate and in the head and nasal cavities. The *EE* vowel lends itself readily to covering, since its normal position requires an intense palatal and head-cavity resonance.

---

2. Phonetic symbols used in the "Description and Execution" heading are from the Webster's and American Heritage systems; the International Phonetic Alphabet is used in the "Common Faults and Corrections" heading.
3. The *IH* vowel is discussed in Lesson 8.
4. Lessons 4, 6, and 7 are studies of fundamental vowels.

In the female voice, it is necessary to *open* all vowels when singing with full voice on high tones. Thus the *EE* vowel, although sung in a closed position in the middle and lower parts of the range, must be opened on the higher notes. The female singer should "think" the *EE* sound on high tones, or her diction will be impaired.

The word *resonance* has been used several times, and for good reason. After breathing, resonance is the most important consideration for the singer. Resonance determines the quality and color of the voice as well as its dynamic range. There are various kinds of resonance:

Induced resonance. A vibrating tuning fork held in the hand can be heard only if held close to the ear. But if the shank of the fork is pressed against a table top, the tone can be heard throughout a large room, since the vibrations from the fork are transmitted to the table top, which then acts as a sounding board. Many musical instruments function through induced vibration. For example, the vibrations from the strings on a violin are conveyed to the body of the instrument, inducing resonance. This "sounding board" effect also functions as we sing. Vibrations that can be felt in the chest when a low tone is sung have been conveyed from the larynx to the ribs and the sternum through the tissues of the neck and the bones of the spinal column.

Sympathetic resonance. Sitting at the piano, depress the damper (right) pedal so that the strings are free to vibrate, then sing various pitches up and down the scale. Soon you will sing a pitch that causes one of the piano strings to vibrate quite audibly. You have sung the pitch to which that particular string is tuned, causing a *sympathetic vibration.*

Cavity resonance. Cavity resonators are tuned resonators; they will respond to only one pitch with maximum resonance. That response is determined by two factors: the size of the cavity and the size of the opening. The larger the cavity, the lower the pitch to which it responds; the larger the opening, the higher the pitch. Thus a low pitch requires a large cavity with a small opening and a high pitch requires a small cavity with a large opening.

If you hold a vibrating tuning fork over the openings of a large variety of bottles, one bottle will greatly amplify the sound. If you then blow over the opening of that bottle, you will find that it produces the same pitch as the fork. If you take a large bottle with a small opening, hold the same vibrating fork at the opening, and gradually fill the bottle with water, eventually the tone will be greatly amplified. What you have done is reduce the volume of the bottle by adding water until its resonance cavity corresponds to the pitch of the fork. (Another example of this form of resonance is the marimba. Its low notes employ long resonating tubes hung under the tuned wooden bars; its high notes have tubes that are small and short.)

The vocal organs, from the larynx (voice box) upwards, can be likened to a kind of organ pipe which branches at the pharynx into two separate pipes, the mouth and the head (see Figure 2–1).

The mouth is the first resonator, producing the primary brilliance of the voice. The head with the nasal cavities is the second, providing a desirable sonorous quality. The chest is a third resonator, which produces sympathetic vibrations below the larynx, providing depth and richness to the tone. We can change the shape of the mouth at will; though we cannot change the shape of the nasal cavities and chest, we can control the extent to which we use them. The effects of all three are present in every tone, but we can control their proportions for purposes of pitch, color, quality, and volume.

The different sounds that we sing are produced by changing the shape of the mouth and the position of the tongue and lips. For example, if we close the mouth we produce a hum. By opening the mouth slightly, raising the front of the tongue, and spreading the lips, the *EE* vowel is produced.

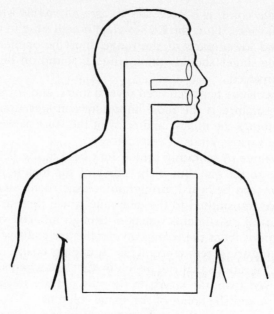

FIGURE 2–1

As has been seen, pitch determines how sound is resonated. A low pitch seeks large resonance cavities (throat, chest, mouth); a high pitch seeks small resonance cavities (in the head, the nasal cavities). Unlike most musical instruments, the voice has adjustable resonators, since we can change the size and the opening of the mouth at will. We can therefore adapt the resonance factors to suit the pitch.

These facts explain why different tongue, lip, and jaw positions must be assumed for each of the sounds that we sing. This, together with the careful "tuning" of all the adjustable resonators of the voice, is of supreme importance in singing, since the weak, simple, almost toneless pitch sent up by the vocal bands must be communicated to all the cavities it can reach and thus resonated into vocal tone. *Evenness of resonance throughout all the pitches in the vocal range must be mastered.*

SONG INTERPRETATION AND MUSICIANSHIP
Handel, "Ombra mai fu" ("Largo")

Memorize the following:

largo: broadly, slow
p (piano): soft
—————— *(crescendo):* increasing power
—————— *(decrescendo):* decreasing power
dolce: sweetly, softly, delicately
': take a breath
mf (mezzo-forte): medium loud
⌒*(fermata):* pause or hold
allarg. (allargando): growing broader (i.e., louder and slower)
f (forte): loud

In the training text, every word is constructed on the *EE* vowel.[5]

Measures 1–15: These measures make up the introduction. Attack the first note of the voice part on pitch; do not attack below the pitch and slide up. Sing lyrically and smoothly, not vigorously or too forcefully.

GENERAL RULE:[6] **Do not waste breath on the first notes of a phrase. Plan phrases to distribute breath evenly.**

Measures 16–17: The combination of crescendo and decrescendo over a single note or group of notes is known as a *messa di voce*. Practice this technique on single notes, then on longer phrases and vocalises (see exercises 3 and 4, this lesson) in order to develop finer control of the breath and voice. Mastery of *messa di voce* is indispensable for superior performance.

GENERAL RULE: Rarely should a long note or phrase be sung without some dynamic variation. Seek to apply $<$, $>$, or $<\ \ >$ to long notes or phrases.

Measure 17: Execute *-neath* as ♩. ♪, not as ♩ ♩ or ♩ ♪.

Measure 18: The word *trees* should be sustained for three full beats and released on beat one of measure 19.

GENERAL RULE: Give all notes full value. Thus a half note (♩) in 2/4 time is released on beat 1 of the following measure; a dotted half note (♩.) in 4/4 time is released on beat 4; a whole note (○) in 4/4 time is released on beat 1. Exceptions will occasionally occur for purposes of breathing and interpretation.

Measure 21: The word *these* must be executed on an even triplet ♩ ♩ ♩, not as ♩ ♩♩, ♩♩♩. or ♩♩. ♩. Do not "scoop" these three notes. If necessary, practice them at first with an aspirate *h* (thee–hee–heez) to avoid sliding and to define the pitch centers. Then eliminate the *h* and merely think it.

GENERAL RULE: Do not adopt the habit of using *h* for purposes of articulation. Clean articulation should be achieved through coordinate action of the diaphragm against the breath. Continued use of the aspirate *h*, which causes a glottal stroke, may eventually damage the voice.

Measure 22: Take a breath at the end of the measure.

Measure 24: On the syllable *-ceives,* do not slide down from E-flat to B-flat. Maintain a similar feeling of head resonance for the lower note as for the upper note.

GENERAL RULE: When notes abruptly drop from high to low, sing the lower note with a sensation of high resonance as on the upper note.

Measure 24: Execute the second B-flat (on *me*) on exactly the same pitch as the first.

---

5. Original texts are also included.

6. Although each *general rule* will be mentioned only once, these principles should be observed in all subsequent songs.

GENERAL RULE: In order not to sing repeated notes flat, imagine a repeated note to be higher than the note it follows.

Measure 26: Release *me* on the second half of beat 2 so that the next phrase may start on beat 3.

GENERAL RULE: New phrases must always start on the proper beat. Time for breathing is taken from the note preceding the new phrase. This is called a "catch breath."

Measure 27: Stress slightly the tied-over E-flat on the first beat in order to bring out the syncopation (displacement of normal accent). Note that this type of tie also occurs in measures 17, 34, and 37.

Measure 43: Slow down the tempo before reaching the fermata (⌢).

GENERAL RULE: Fermatas are frequently approached with a *ritardando*.

Measure 45: Observe the *allargando*.

Measures 47–52: These measures are the postlude.

This song is from the first act of the opera *Xerxes*.

Ombra mai fu

Largo

George Frideric Handel
(1685–1759)

1. *Training text:* Be - neath these — trees.
2. *Italian text:* Om - bra mai — fu

me,   re – ceives_____ me.

più,   *so – a – ve più.*

The *EH* Vowel

Webster's New World:	e
American Heritage:	ĕ
International:	ɛ

WORDS WITH THE *EH* VOWEL

Read aloud slowly:

Ned	fed	wed	many
wet	lend	let	bread
went	Bess	met	weather
quest	end	said	send

Sing:

1. Very slowly.

Ned	fed	wed	wet	lend	bread	went	let
Bess	met	quest	end	said	send	fret	west

2. Very slowly.

Ned	fed	wed	wet	lend
Bess	met	quest	end	said

3. Very slowly; sing with one breath.

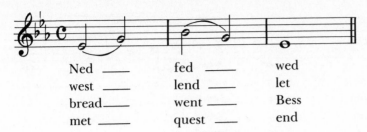

Ned ____	fed ____	wed
west ____	lend ____	let
bread____	went ____	Bess
met ____	quest ___	end

4. Moderately; sing with one breath

Ned_____	fed _____	wed _____	west
lend_____	let _____	bread_____	went
Bess _____	met _____	quest _____	end
said _____	send_____	fend _____	bend

SENTENCES WITH THE *EH* VOWEL

Sing until all *EH* vowels are clearly executed.

1. Very slowly; sing with one breath.

ⓐ Ned's	guest	went	west.
ⓑ Ten	men	met	death.
ⓒ "Well!"	said	fair	Nell.
ⓓ Seth	fed	Ted	bread.

2. Very slowly.

ⓐ Ned's	guest	went	west.	ⓑ Ten	men	met	death.
ⓒ "Well!"	said	fair	Nell.	ⓓ Seth	fed	Ted	bread.

3. Moderately; sing with one breath.

ⓐ Ned's ____	guest __	went __	west.
ⓑ Ten ____	men __	met __	death.
ⓒ "Well!"____	said __	fair __	Nell.
ⓓ Seth ____	fed __	Ted __	bread.

4. Moderately; sing with one breath.

ⓐ Ned's _____	guest	went __ west. _____
ⓑ Ten _____	men	met __ death. _____
ⓒ "Well!" _____	said	fair __ Nell. _____
ⓓ Seth _____	fed	Ted __ bread. _____

STUDY

The *EH* (e, ĕ) Vowel:
Description and Execution

The *EH* vowel is an open, bright, front vowel. *EH* is sung as follows:

1. The front of the tongue is raised.
2. The tip of the tongue is forward.
3. The upper lip is raised in a smiling position.
4. The jaw is down in a relaxed position.

The *EH* (ɛ) Vowel:
Common Faults and Corrections

Singers often substitute *IH* for *EH*, singing *sinned* instead of *send*, *pin* instead of *pen*, and *inny* instead of *any*. (See Lesson 8 for a thorough discussion of the *IH* vowel.) *EH* should be sung more open than *IH*. Practice speaking and then singing the following words in sequence:

EE (i)	*IH* (ɪ)	*EH* (ɛ)
me	miss	met
fee	fit	fell
be	bit	bed
leap	lip	led

When singing *EH*, do not tense the lower lip, tighten the jaw, or pull at the corners of the mouth. Simply drop the jaw in a relaxed, comfortable manner.

General Principles of Singing

Phoneticians classify vowels as *open* or *closed*, depending on the relative size of the mouth opening. In addition, vowel sounds are classified as either *front* or *back*, according to the position of the tongue. The front of the tongue (not the tip) is higher for the front vowels; the back of the tongue is higher for the back vowels.

Vowels are also classified on the basis of their quality or color. A vowel may be *bright* or *dark*, according to its characteristic type of resonance. All front vowels are classified as bright, and back vowels are classified as dark. *EH* and *EE* are front, bright vowels, because the front of the tongue is raised when they are sung and because of their high proportion of palatal and head-cavity resonance.

Open vowels tend to be resonated farther back in the mouth and throat than are closed vowels. But both open and closed vowels must have palatal and head resonance; these are necessary for *projection*, production of tone which has carrying power.

Each vowel sound requires its own individual quality. Nothing is so dull as a voice that has neutralized all vowels into one consistently bright or dark color. All qualities of the various vowel sounds should be used. As the student becomes proficient, he or she should learn to color each vowel according to the meaning of the text. For example, joy or happiness often requires a bright vowel color, death or lamentation a darker color. Listen to recordings of fine singers and notice how they color the vowels in order to enhance their interpretation.

Classification of voices.   Voices are divided into four general classes: soprano, alto, tenor, and bass. Various subdivisions, denoting the quality or style of the voice, occur within these classifications and are widely recognized and accepted in the United States.

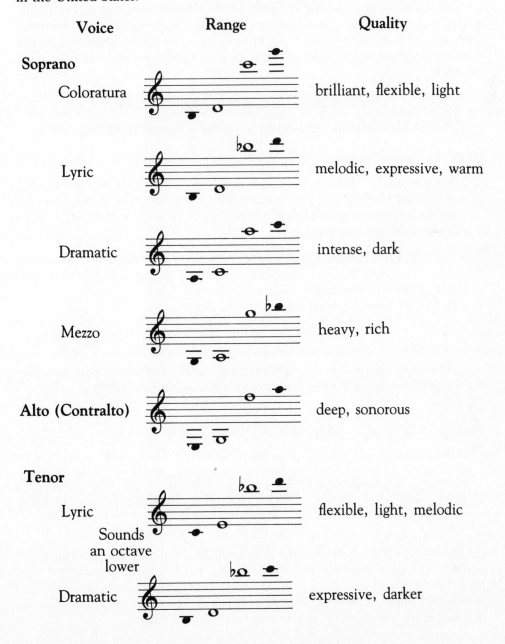

Voice	Range	Quality
Soprano		
Coloratura		brilliant, flexible, light
Lyric		melodic, expressive, warm
Dramatic		intense, dark
Mezzo		heavy, rich
Alto (Contralto)		deep, sonorous
Tenor		
Lyric		flexible, light, melodic
Sounds an octave lower		
Dramatic		expressive, darker

Bass

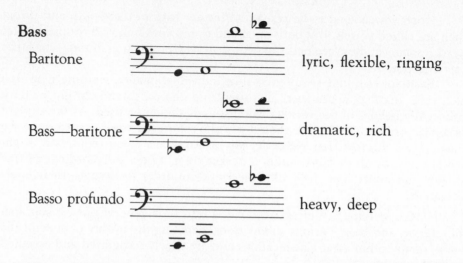

Baritone — lyric, flexible, ringing

Bass—baritone — dramatic, rich

Basso profundo — heavy, deep

All classifications depend on quality and *tessitura* (general pitch position) as well as *range* (total span from lowest pitch to the highest pitch). It sometimes takes several years of voice study before the voice can be classified. Beginning students must use their voices properly so that vocal development will not be impeded.

SONG INTERPRETATION AND MUSICIANSHIP

Claudio Monteverdi, "Lasciatemi morire" ("Lamento di Arianna")

Memorize the following:

> *lento:* slow
> *più f:* more loudly
> *affrett.* (affrettando): hurrying; hurried
> *riten. molto* (ritenuto molto): much slower

Hum and then sing this song in a legato style. The training text has many *EE* and *EH* vowels. Make certain that you sing the rhythmic figure ♪ ♪ in measures 12 and 14 accurately.

This is a three-part song form:

	A	B	A
measures	1–7	8–15	16–20

The vocal range of this song is relatively small. The lowest note is E, the highest is D. Counting E as 1, there are six more scale steps to D:

1 2 3 4 5 6 7

Thus we say this song has a vocal range of a seventh. Study other songs and determine their vocal ranges. The wider the range, the more difficult the song is likely to be. "The Star Spangled Banner," for example, has a vocal range of a twelfth.

Claudio Monteverdi was one of the greatest Italian composers of the late Renaissance and early Baroque. During the latter part of his life, from 1613 to 1643, he was *maestro di cappella* at St. Marks in Venice. He wrote huge quantities of religious music, madrigals, operas, and ballets. The "Lament of Arianna" is the only music preserved from a lost opera entitled *L'Arianna*.

Lasciatemi morire

Lamento di Arianna

Claudio Monteverdi
(1567–1643)

1. *Training text:* Let death, _____ let death be-
2. *Italian text:* La - scia - - te - mi mo -

friend me! Let death, let death _____ be-friend me!
ri - re! La - scia - te - mi _____ mo - ri - re!

What, I do beg thee, _____ could lend me
E che vo - le - - te, _____ che mi con -

The *AH* Vowel

Webster's New World:	ä
American Heritage:	ä
International:	*a*

WORDS WITH THE *AH* VOWEL

Read aloud slowly:

ma	farm	heart	far
ark	charm	mar	calm
barb	harm	march	dark
bar	dart	jar	psalm

Sing:

1. Very slowly.

| ma | ark | barb | bar | car | dark | far | farm |
| charm | harm | dart | calm | garb | guard | heart | mar |

2. Very slowly.

| ma | charm | march | arch | heart |
| ark | harm | jar | palm | mar |

3. Very slowly; sing with one breath.

large	mart	mark
Marge	smart	marsh
ma	car	dark
calm	garb	farm

4. Moderately; sing with one breath.

ma	ark	barb	ma
car	dark	far	car
charm	harm	dart	charm
garb	guard	heart	garb

SENTENCES WITH THE *AH* VOWEL

Sing until all *AH* vowels are clearly produced.

1. Very slowly.

ⓐ Mark's	farm	was	large.
ⓑ The	arch	was	large.
ⓒ These	parks	are	dark.
ⓓ Blest	are	sweet	hearts.

2. Very slowly.

| ⓐ Weak | hearts | seek | calm. | ⓑ Large | yards | need | seed. |
| ⓒ These | bees | are | calm. | ⓓ We | see | Ted's | need. |

3. Moderately; sing with one breath.

ⓐ Mark's	farm - was	large.
ⓑ The	arch - was	large.
ⓒ These	parks - are	dark.
ⓓ Blest	are sweet - hearts.

4. Moderately; sing with one breath.

ⓐ Mark's_____	farm	was___	large._____
ⓑ The_____	arch	was___	large._____
ⓒ These_____	parks	are___	dark._____
ⓓ Blest_____	are	sweet - hearts._____

STUDY

The *AH* (ä) Vowel: Description and Execution

The *AH* vowel is the most open of all vowels, the lowest of all the back vowels. The fundamental *AH* is often followed by the consonant *r* and is executed as follows:

1. The tip of the tongue is forward, touching the back of the lower front teeth. The tongue lies relatively flat.
2. The jaw is dropped, but relaxed.
3. The lips are rounded easily forward.

The *AH* (ɑ) Vowel: Common Faults and Corrections

As noted in Lesson 3, it is difficult for students to achieve enough head resonance on back vowels. The *AH* vowel presents such a problem, for students tend to "swallow" the sound. The visible result of this is an artificially lowered larynx and lips that are too protuberant (sometimes called "trumpet lips"). The aural result is a dull, thick, guttural tone. To avoid this, speak and then sing a sequence of words beginning with a front vowel, proceeding through others which tend to resonate farther back in the mouth and chest. The goal is to keep the second sound as resonant as the first, the third as resonant as the second, and so on. Thus:

EE (i) —— *EH* (ε) —— *AH* (a)
We —— met —— smart
She —— dealt —— cards

Apply this principle to the exercises at the beginning of the lesson. Note that *AH* is represented by the spelling *a* in all the words studied in this lesson. Some *AH* words, however, are spelled with *o*: *odd, hot, box, cop, God, lot, rot,* and *pot.* Do not substitute the vowels *AW* (see Lesson 6) or *ĂH* (see Lesson 5).

General Principles of Singing

As students begin to sing solos in public, if only in front of the voice class, they should become concerned with stage deportment. Effectiveness as a singer depends not only upon one's voice and choice of songs, but also upon a good platform manner.

When singing, one should be poised, with an air of dignity and sincerity. If one appears ill at ease, the audience will respond in kind. Modest assurance is the ideal manner, and nothing begets assurance like intelligent practice and vocal skill. Certain standard procedures of stage etiquette should be observed:

1. A woman usually precedes a man on and off the stage, regardless of which is the accompanist or soloist. When both accompanist and soloist are of the same sex, the soloist enters and leaves first.
2. The soloist's entrance is made with a quick but graceful walk to a definite spot, usually the crook of the piano.
3. If the singer is greeted by applause, he or she should acknowledge it with a graceful bow upon reaching the desired spot: one foot is placed behind the other, the weight is shifted to the rear foot, and the body is bent forward slightly from the waist. The bow should fit the singer's personality and physique.
4. What to do with the hands is a problem for many singers. The custom is to hold the hands together at the waist. Raising and extending them while singing produces an unnatural and affected appearance. Posing and affectation are for singers who do not have talent enough to do without them.
5. When the audience is quiet and ready to listen, a slight nod is given to the accompanist as a signal to begin.
6. During introductions and interludes, the soloist maintains an attentive attitude.
7. The mood of the song should be reflected in the general manner of singing. One voice teacher has said that the singer should "look like the music."
8. When singing, the soloist looks above the heads of the audience and does not stare fixedly at one spot. He or she avoids glancing about in a nervous, restless manner.
9. When singing as a soloist with an orchestra or chorus, the one unforgivable sin is to make a mistake because of not watching the conductor.
10. At the end of a song, the soloist should not bow before the applause begins.
11. An encore should not be sung unless the applause calls for one.

The best way to learn good stage deportment is by observing seasoned professional singers.

SONG INTERPRETATION AND MUSICIANSHIP

Giordani "Caro mio ben" ("Ah! My Dear Heart")

The tempo mark *Andante con moto* means "walking" or "moderately slow," "with motion."

Memorize the following:

rit. (ritardando): delaying the time gradually

più: more

poco: little

accel. (accelerando): gradually increasing the speed of the movement

e: and

port. (portamento) (from *portare,* meaning "to carry"): indicates a carrying or gliding of the tone from one note to the next, but so rapidly that the intermediate notes are not defined.

a tempo: in time; signifies that after some deviation or relaxation of the tempo, the performer must return to the regular tempo.

The training text of this song has been made up almost entirely of words constructed on the *EE, EH,* and *AH* vowels.

Measure 3: The figure ♪♪. must not be executed as ♩⌐♪. Feel the sixteenth note (♪) as belonging to the following half note (♩) rather than to the preceding ♪. ♪ figure.

Measure 6: Practice this measure daily to develop flexibility in performing the grace notes (short appoggiaturas).

Measure 13: Increase speed; prepare to slow down on the last two beats of measure 14.

Measures 13–19: Note the considerable variation in both tempo and dynamics. Rehearse the following separately:

1. Practice the tempo changes only *(poco accel., più allargando, a tempo).* At first, exaggerate these shifts, in order to make yourself more conscious of the changes. When fully aware of them, work toward more subtle contrasts in tempo.
2. Practice the dynamic changes ($\longleftarrow$ $\longrightarrow$) in steady tempo. At first, exaggerate these changes as well, then work toward more musical dynamic variation.

Measures 19–20: Note the *portamento.* Glide from A to D in measure 20 without giving definition to the intermediate pitches. Do not take a breath between these notes.

Although students are urged to continue through this book step by step, exploring the characteristics of one sound at a time, some may wish to extend their vocal experience beyond the songs in each lesson. To this purpose, twenty-two additional songs are included at the end of the book. The first of these is a German folk song, "Da unten im Tale" ("Below in the Valley"), arranged by Johannes Brahms. Brahms is well known for his four great symphonies and for other compositions in large forms. Less known are the 166 songs for solo voice, the many duets, the large volume of works for male, female, and mixed chorus, and the numerous choral/orchestral works. He was devoted to German folk music; "Below in the Valley" is one of 105 published arrangements of folk songs. Sing this little song, which is in strophic form, with the utmost simplicity and sincerity.

In the eighteenth century, ornamental interpolations were a customary practice among singers. Performing such interpolations called for a high degree of technical skill from the performer and reflected his or her virtuosity. Although "Caro mio ben" is a relatively simple example of eighteenth-century song, it requires the embellished style. At the discretion of the teacher, this should include trills, appoggiaturas, and the general "filling up" of intervals at appropriate places.

Caro mio ben
Ah! My Dear Heart

Giuseppe Giordani
(1753–1798)

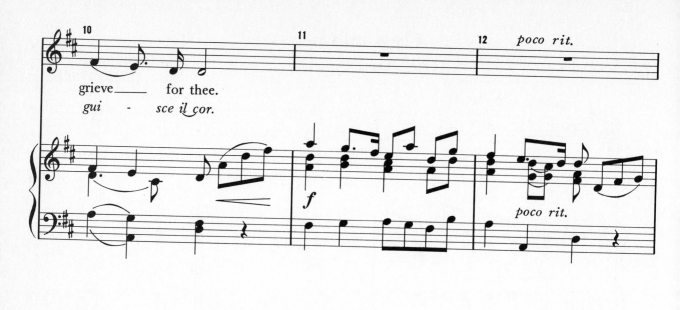

I grieve for thee.

lan - gui - sce il cor.

The A͝H Vowel

Webster's New World:	a
American Heritage:	ă
International:	æ

WORDS WITH THE A͝H VOWEL

Read aloud slowly:

	Pure		*Diphthongs*[1]
man	dance	last	I
can	mask	chance	my
ran	fast	can't	sigh
an	past	laugh	fine

Sing

1. Very slowly.

man	sand	mask	band	Ann	am	laugh	I
can	had	fast	bad	path	fine	sigh	my

2. Very slowly.

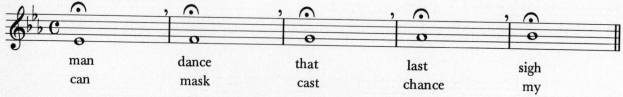

man	dance	that	last	sigh
can	mask	cast	chance	my

---

1. For a full discussion of the diphthongized A͝H, see Lesson 10.

3. Very slowly; sing with one breath.

man_____	can _____	fine
an _____	sigh_____	had
and_____	dance_____	I
fast_____	my_____	ask

4. Moderately; sing with one breath.

Ann_____	can't _____	my _____	fine
past _____	path _____	laugh_____	sigh
sand _____	ask _____	mast _____	glass
prance_____	had _____	band _____	half

SENTENCES WITH THE *A͞H* VOWEL

Sing until all vowels are clearly produced.

1. Very slowly; sing with one breath.

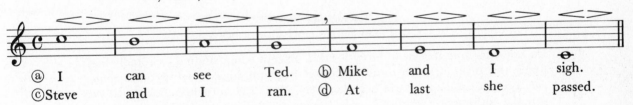

ⓐ Can	that	man_____	laugh?
ⓑ Mike	and	Bess _____	sigh.
ⓒ We	like	that_____	band.
ⓓ That	fat	man_____	passed.

2. Very slowly.

| ⓐ I | can | see | Ted. | ⓑ Mike | and | I | sigh. |
| ⓒ Steve | and | I | ran. | ⓓ At | last | she | passed. |

3. Moderately; sing with one breath.

ⓐ Can_____	that__ man__	laugh?
ⓑ I_____	can__ see __	Ted.
ⓒ We_____	like__ that__	band.
ⓓ That_____	fat __ man__	passed.

4.   Moderately; sing with one breath.

ⓐ	She_____	can	laugh__	last._____
ⓑ	Mike_____	and	Bess __	dance._____
ⓒ	Steve_____	and	I ___	sigh._____
ⓓ	At_____	last	she __	passed._____

STUDY

The *ĂH (a, ă)* Vowel:
Description and Execution

The *ĂH* vowel is an open, front vowel. It is the lowest of the front vowel sounds—that is, the tongue is lower than for any other front vowel. The term *medial* is sometimes used to denote this vowel's place between the front, bright *EH* sound and the back dark *AH* sound.

The *ĂH* vowel does not appear in either Italian or German; thus it is often overlooked by singers trained exclusively in European literature. It is always spelled with the letter *a* except in diphthongs, and appears in stressed syllables more frequently than any other *a* in the English language.

The *i* sound is produced when *ĂH* is combined with *IH* to form a diphthong *(mine, vine, I)*. The vowel is sung the same whether it is pure or it forms the first part of a diphthong.

To sing *ĂH* correctly:

1.   The tip of the tongue touches the lower front teeth.
2.   The front of the tongue is only slightly arched and is lower than for *EE* and EH.
3.   The jaw is dropped less than for the more open fundamental *AH.*
4.   The lips are in a smiling position.

The *ĂH (æ)* Vowel:
Common Faults and Corrections

Do not substitute *AH* (as in *farm*) for *ĂH.* Except when singing extremely high tones, this pronunciation sounds affected and unnatural: *hand* becomes *hahnd, man* becomes *mahn,* and *can* becomes *cahn.* Your ear must help you avoid this mistake, although certain mechanical means will also help. Widen the sides of the tongue and the corners of the mouth. Keep the soft palate high (check with a hand mirror) or a distressing nasal twang may result; this applies particularly to words like *France, dance,* and *prance.* It may be helpful to approach *ĂH* through *AH* by slowly speaking and then singing the following words in sequence:

EH (ε)	*AH*(a)	*ĂH* (æ)
met	mart	mad
help	heart	had
let	lard	lad
bet	bard	bad

Keep the soft palate as high for A͞H as for *EH* and *AH*.

Do not substitute *EH* for A͞H in words which have the consonant *r* or *rr;* otherwise, *marry* becomes *merry*, *Paris* becomes *Perris*, *Carol* becomes *Cerol*, and *paradise* becomes *peradise*. Speak and sing these words until you can avoid this mistake.

General Principles of Singing

Avoiding mistakes depends on a trained ear. Hearing plays just as important a part in singing as do observation and technique. One may observe good singers and build one's own technique, but the final result is dependent upon one's ability to *hear* what beautiful tone and expression are.

We study singing to build a technique through which to express songs. Everyone agrees that expressiveness is paramount, and that technique by itself is almost worthless. But expression without technique is impossible. Singers must enlarge their powers of expression, their ability to project, and their understanding of style, phrasing, and nuance, while building their technique. These are principles of singing upon which all knowledgeable musicians agree.

SONG INTERPRETATION AND MUSICIANSHIP
Franz, "Dedication" ("Widmung")

The tempo is marked *Andante espressivo*, which approximately means "flowing easily, with expression."

Memorize the following:

(in piano part): arpeggio; ripple the notes of a chord in harp style. The arpeggio begins on the beat and starts with the lowest note.

The training text of this song consists almost entirely of words constructed on the *EE*, *EH*, *AH*, and A͝H vowels.

Fine music is usually organized in passages of notes that are related melodically, harmonically, and rhythmically. These passages, often four or eight measures long, are called *phrases*. When learning songs, always think in terms of the phrase rather than of individual notes. Most phrases have a rise and fall in dynamics, as does the first phrase of this song. Most phrases climax on a note or group of notes; the approach to and departure from these climaxes must be carefully planned. Each phrase must also relate to other phrases so that, when combined, they form a logical, artistic whole. To phrase properly, one should be conscious of:

Text.   The relative importance of the individual words, as well as the mood they are projecting, must be understood. It is often helpful to recite the text alone, speaking it as an actor would. Once it is understood, it should be sung with the same expression as when recited.

Melody.   Melodic lines usually have a curve or arch, which creates a feeling of tension as the phrase climax approaches and a feeling of relaxation as it recedes. Sensitivity to this ebb and flow in the melodic line will make one's singing more intelligible and musical.

Harmony.   The accompaniment is a vital aid to the singer's phrasing. Harmonies and pianistic patterns give hints as to dynamic and tempo variations, mood, and word stress.

Analyze "Dedication" with your teacher and other singers. Note that each phrase has been marked with a slur (⌒). Make each phrase meaningful both by itself and as a part of the song. Here are some questions to answer about each phrase.

1. What are the key words?
2. What are the "mood" or "color" words?
3. How wide is the dynamic range? (Is the < > in measure 2 the same as those in measure 5 or measures 11–12?)
4. Are there phrases that speed up or slow down?
5. Where is the *melodic* climax? Does the harmony in the accompaniment help to determine this?
6. Where is the *dynamic* climax?
7. How does phrase 1 relate to phrase 2? How do these relate to other phrases?
8. Where is the climax of the song? Has it been properly prepared by the phrases leading to it? If the climax is not at the end, how are the measures following it to be sung?

Although outstanding singers leave some of their artistry to the inspiration of the moment, most great and true expression is the result of painstaking effort and thoughtful planning. Analyze the songs you have previously learned in a similar way.

On page 191 may be found another lovely song with many *ĂH* vowels— "My Lovely Celia" by George Monro. This strophic song should be sung very simply but with expression. Practice the florid passages slowly at first, making sure the vowels are pure. Observe the dynamic markings carefully. Do not make the mistake of taking the words too seriously; approach them with tongue-in-cheek humor. George Monro was an eighteenth-century organist and composer. Like many secular songs of this period, "My Lovely Celia" is about unrequited love.

Robert Franz is one of the most important composers of the German lied. His compositions and arrangements include 257 songs with piano accompaniment (in 45 sets), all of which were composed originally for mezzo-soprano. He did not write dramatic ballads; he excluded from his songs all that was passionate or extreme in feeling.

Dedication

Widmung

Wolfgang Muller

Robert Franz
(1815–1892)

Andante espressivo

1. Training text: Ah! thank me not for that I sing thee; I ask thee
2. German text: O dan - ke nicht für die - se Lie - der, mir ziemt es,

thanks, these songs are thine. They came from thee,_____
dank - bar dir zu sein; Du gabst sie mir,_____

Thy hand the giv - er and thine a - lone shall al - ways
ich ge - be wie - der, was jetzt und einst und e - wig

Dost thou not know____ that these____ are thine?____
kennst du die eig - nen Lie - der nicht?____

Dost thou not know____ that these____ are thine?____
Kennst du die eig - nen Lie - der nicht?____

The *AW* Vowel

Webster's New World:	ô
American Heritage:	ô
International:	ɔ

WORDS WITH THE *AW* VOWEL

Read aloud slowly:

all	drawl	jaw	mall
awe	fawn	law	yawn
ball	fall	lawn	pause
paw	Gaul	Maud	raw

Sing:

1. Very slowly.

all	cause	fawn	haul	lawn	talk	raw	song
awe	call	fall	hawk	Maud	yawl	warm	thought

2. Very slowly.

talk	yawl	yawn	pause	raw
song	thought	long	cause	gone

3. Very slowly; sing with one breath.

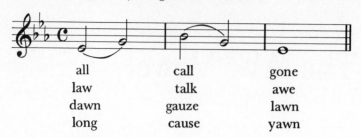

all	call	gone
law	talk	awe
dawn	gauze	lawn
long	cause	yawn

4. Moderately; sing with one breath.

all _____	cause _____	fawn _____	haul
lawn _____	talk _____	raw _____	awe
call _____	law _____	hawk _____	maul
dog _____	gone _____	long _____	song

SENTENCES WITH THE *AW* VOWEL

Sing until all vowels are clearly produced.

1. Very slowly.

ⓐ Long	talks	cause _____	yawns.
ⓑ Seek	God	be _____	calm.
ⓒ Call	my	boss, _____	Maud.
ⓓ She	longs	for _____	song.

2. Very slowly.

| ⓐ Ball | parks | are | vast | ⓑ We | can | all | fall |
| ⓒ Dogs | leap | on | lawns. | ⓓ He | hauled | that e | tar. |

3. Moderately; sing with one breath.

ⓐ Long _____	talks _ cause _	yawns.
ⓑ Seek _____	God _ be _	calm.
ⓒ Call _____	my _ boss, _	Maud.
ⓓ She _____	longs _ for _	song.

4. Moderately; sing with one breath.

ⓐ Ball_____	parks	are___	vast _____
ⓑ We_____	can	all___	fall._____
ⓒ Dogs_____	leap	on ___	lawns._____
ⓓ He_____	hauled	that ___	tar._____

STUDY

The *AW* (ô) Vowel:
Description and Execution

The *AW* vowel is an open vowel. Like *AH* (as in *farm*), it is a back vowel, but much darker. *AW* is produced as follows:

1. The back of the tongue is raised in an arched position, slightly higher than for *AH*.
2. The tip of the tongue is forward.
3. The lips are pursed, forming an oval shape. The corners of the mouth are drawn easily toward each other. The jaw is dropped.

The *AW* (ɔ) Vowel:
Common Faults and Corrections

In some sections of the country, *AH* is mistakenly substituted for *AW* in most words. Singers should change this localized pronunciation to standard pronunciation. Words in which this substitution is most likely to occur are those which contain the letters: *al, ald, alk, all, alt, au, aught,* and *aw*. Practice speaking and singing the following words, using *AW*, not *AH*.

also	bald	talk[1]	call	salt	cause	taught	law
always	scald	walk[1]	ball	exalt	fault	daughter	saw

General Principles of Singing

In all the lessons up to this point, the legato style—the linking together of words—has been emphasized. Even in songs which are to be sung mostly legato, however, there are phrases within which words should not be joined. Three rules concern phrases of this kind:

1. When a word ends in the same vowel sound with which the next word begins, the words must be separated. For example, sing "the / east," not "theeast," and "the / eve," not "theeve."

This rule also applies to diphthongs. Thus: "say / it," not "sayit," because the *EH* vowel in *say* ends with *IH*, the same sound that begins *it*. This rule applies only when the *sound* is the same. When the sounds are different, even when spelled with the same letter, the words are usually connected.

---

1. The letter *l* in these words is silent.

2. Whenever diction may be obscured, the words must be separated. For example, if each pair of words on the left below are not separated, they will produce a sound like the words on the right.

round /eyes	dies
whose / eyes	sighs
name / any	many
prayer / O	row

Exceptions to this rule are determined by the relative importance of the words within a phrase. In the phrase "O Lord of Hosts," the word *Lord* is so important, and the word *of* so unimportant, that "Lord of" can be connected without fear of loss of meaning. On the other hand, in the phrase "Let us pray" the important word is *pray*. If *us* is connected with *pray,* the invitation will seem to be "Let us spray!"

3. To heighten the dramatic effect of a word beginning with a vowel, the words are separated by means of stress on the vowel. For example, sing:

O / endless / agony! (stress *e*ndless *a*gony)
He is / ill! (stress *i*ll)
Where / are you? (stress *a*re)

This rule applies only in situations that require dramatic effect.

SONG INTERPRETATION AND MUSICIANSHIP

Bohm, "Calm as the Night" ("Still wie die Nacht")

The tempo is marked *tranquillo,* which means restful and quiet.
Memorize the following:

⌒
········· (piano part): semi-legato

The training text includes many *AW* vowels.
Throughout this volume, each song introduces or emphasizes a technical problem pertaining to either vowels or consonants. In studying these songs, it is helpful at first to sing the melodies with neutral syllables rather than the text provided. Neutral syllables are combinations of vowels and consonants which can be used for vocalization *(mee, meh, mah, maw).* They can be helpful in isolating a vowel or consonant problem. For example, this song could be sung first on the neutral syllable *maw* if the student is having difficulty with the *AW* sound. Use neutral syllables for all songs throughout this volume.

Measure 11: Always return to the original tempo after singing the *ritardando.* Singers tend to return to a tempo slower than the original after a *ritardando.*

Measure 36: Do not sing *the* on the sixth beat of the measure; it occurs on the *second half* of the sixth beat. Think of it as being connected to *night* rather than to *as.*

Measure 37: The same rhythm is encountered at the word *and*.

Measures 36–39: Do not strain or force the voice. This phrase has a high tessitura and is quite demanding.[2] Sing no louder than you can sing with good tone. Remember the *con moto*.

Observe the breath marks throughout this song. Plan each phrase so that breath is distributed evenly. Breath marks are omitted where rests appear.

As a supplementary song for this lesson, try the lovely southern mountain tune "He's Gone Away" on page 194. Sing with great simplicity and freedom. Note that there are measures which are uneven in length ($\frac{4}{4}$ $\frac{3}{4}$ $\frac{4}{4}$ $\frac{2}{4}$). Keep the length of the quarter note the same in all these measures. The accompaniment has been arranged for piano, but you may wish to sing this song with guitar accompaniment. If played well, this can be most effective.

This song was written by the German pianist and salon composer Carl Bohm. It is his best-known composition and has long been a favorite among both professional and amateur singers.

---

2.   For many young voices, the teacher may wish to transpose this song into the key of B♭ or A♭.

Calm as the Night

Still wie die Nacht

Carl Bohm
(1844—1920)

1. *Training text:* Calm as the night, strong as the sea,
2. *German text:* Still wie die Nacht, tief wie das Meer,

Thus is my love for thee.
soll dei - ne Lie - be sein!

If love calls thee,
Wenn du mich liebst

As love called me,_____ Thine shall I al - ways
so wie ich dich,_____ will ich dein ei - gen

be. Calm_____ as the night,_____ and
sein. Heiss_____ wie der Stahl,_____ und

Strong as the Sea, Thus all my love,___ my___
fest wie der Stein soll dei - ne Lie - be, dei - ne

love___ shall be.___ Thus all my love___ shall
Lie - be sein,___ soll dei - ne Lie - be

be.___
sein!___

The $\overline{OO}$ Vowel

Webster's New World:	$\overline{oo}$
American Heritage:	$\overline{oo}$
International:	u

WORDS WITH THE $\overline{OO}$ VOWEL

Read aloud slowly:

soon	noon	rue	boom
cool	broom	to	lose
too	plume	loom	loop
shoe	food	who	through

Sing:

1. Very slowly.

soon	do	plume	juice	rue	lose	room	doom
tool	fool	food	to	move	loop	through	flute

2. Very slowly.

soon	cool	tool	too	rue
do	shoe	fool	noon	broom

3. Very slowly; sing with one breath.

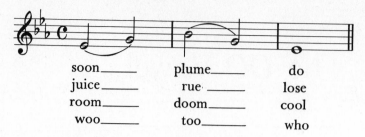

soon_____	plume_____	do
juice_____	rue_____	lose
room_____	doom_____	cool
woo_____	too_____	who

4. Moderately; sing with one breath.

soon_____	plume_____	rue_____	room
cool_____	you_____	coo_____	mood
tool_____	food_____	move_____	through
shoe_____	goose_____	soothe_____	brood

The vocalises to this point have been the same in each lesson. For variety, and to introduce students to minor keys, sentences in this and the next four lessons will be based on different vocalises. Number 1 (p. 63) introduces C minor; students will note that the key signature is the same as for E-flat major. Relative minor scales always begin a third below their relative major and have the same key signature. Here is a chart of all the major keys and their relative minor keys. Memorize the chart. Go back to each song studied so far and determine its key. Do this for all songs in the future.

Major Keys		Relative Minor Keys	Major Keys		Relative Minor Keys
F	𝄞♭	d	G	𝄞♯	e
B♭	𝄞♭♭	g	D	𝄞♯♯	b
E♭	𝄞♭♭♭	c	A	𝄞♯♯♯	f♯
A♭	𝄞♭♭♭♭	f	E	𝄞♯♯♯♯	c♯
D♭	𝄞♭♭♭♭♭	b♭	B	𝄞♯♯♯♯♯	g♯

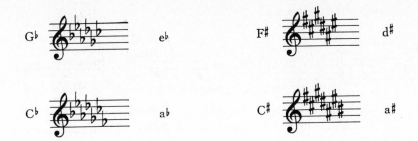

Note that in exercise 2, measures 4–5, there is a B-natural. When the seventh pitch in a minor scale is raised, as here, the scale is called a *harmonic minor* scale. In exercise 4, measure 1, both A and B are natural, while in measure 3, both are flatted. When the sixth and seventh pitches of a minor scale are raised going up and lowered going down, as here, the scale is called a *melodic minor* scale. When no pitches are altered, the scale is called a *natural minor* scale

SENTENCES WITH THE $\overline{OO}$ VOWEL

Sing until all $\overline{OO}$ vowels are clearly executed.

1. Very slowly.

ⓐ Sue _____ crooned _____ "Blue _____ Moon."
ⓑ Luke's _____ suit _____ grew _____ loose.
ⓒ Ice _____ cools _____ fruit _____ juice.
ⓓ Whose _____ suit _____ fits _____ you?

2. Very slowly.

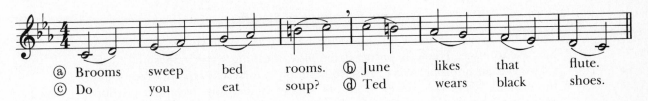

ⓐ Brooms sweep bed rooms. ⓑ June likes that flute.
ⓒ Do you eat soup? ⓓ Ted wears black shoes.

3. Moderately.

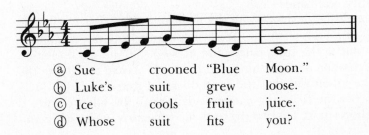

ⓐ Sue crooned "Blue Moon."
ⓑ Luke's suit grew loose.
ⓒ Ice cools fruit juice.
ⓓ Whose suit fits you?

4.   Sing with one breath.

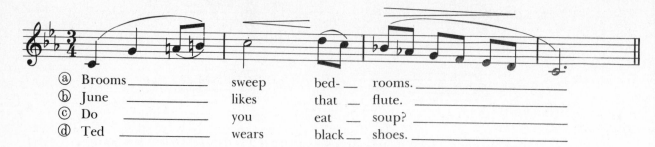

   ⓐ Brooms_____ sweep   bed-__ rooms._____
   ⓑ June _____ likes   that __ flute. _____
   ⓒ Do   _____ you   eat __   soup?_____
   ⓓ Ted   _____ wears   black__ shoes. _____

STUDY

The $\overline{OO}$ (oo) Vowel:
Description and Execution

The $\overline{OO}$ vowel is the most closed of all vowels. It is the highest of all the dark, back vowels.

Sing $\overline{OO}$ as follows:

1.   The back of the tongue is arched toward the soft palate.
2.   The tip of the tongue touches the lower front teeth.
3.   The lips are rounded forward to a small opening about the size of the tip of the little finger.

Keep the sides of the lips narrow so that they form a circle, not a slit. Do not pull the upper lip downward; allow it to protrude well away from the teeth.

The $\overline{OO}$ (u) Vowel:
Common Faults and Corrections

Do not allow $\overline{OO}$ to sound "swallowed" or "hooty," a condition caused by opening the mouth too much, creating too high a proportion of resonance in the throat and chest. Round the lips forward so that they are almost closed. Concentrate $\overline{OO}$ resonance in the mouth and head and nasal cavities.

General Principles of Singing

The $\overline{OO}$ vowel is an excellent sound for helping the male student to develop his falsetto voice. The term *falsetto* (from *falso*, meaning "false") does not imply that this is an improper voice; falsetto is simply a different type of voice from the normal, "full" male voice. When one sings falsetto, only the upper portion of the vocal bands phonate (look back at Figure 1–7F), and almost all resonance is in the head and nasal cavities. Moreover, the vocal bands are not completely closed, a position which gives the falsetto its soft, almost breathy quality. A smooth crescendo from falsetto to full voice is impossible, since a "break" in the voice occurs when the vocal bands close.

The falsetto should be developed by the male singer, since it is valuable for singing passages in a high tessitura. In developing the falsetto, resonate a high proportion of tone at the hard palate and in the head and nasal cavities. There should be a sensation of "breathing into the tone." Learn to balance the breath allotted to the falsetto so that the tone does not sound breathy. Male students should practice the following exercises daily until the falsetto voice is secured. *Caution:* Always start falsetto practice on extremely high notes and work down.

Sing at actual pitch.

Loo, Loo, Loo, Loo, Loo,   Loo, Loo, Loo, Loo, Loo,   Loo, Loo, Loo, Loo, Loo,   etc.

Loo, Loo, Loo, Loo, Loo,   Loo, Loo, Loo, Loo, Loo,   Loo, Loo, Loo, Loo, Loo,   etc.

poo_____   mee eh ah   mee eh ah   etc.

SONG INTERPRETATION AND MUSICIANSHIP

Schubert, "Wanderer's Night Song" ("Wanderers Nachtlied")

The tempo is marked *lento,* which means "slowly." *Lento* is often used to indicate a temporary slowness; in this song, however, it represents the tempo throughout. The song should be sung with a feeling of restfulness and quiet.

The training text contains many words having the $\overline{OO}$ vowel sound.

Note that both staves of the accompaniment are in the bass clef. There are many sixteenth notes (♪ ♪) and ♩. ♪ figures in this song. All too often, singers perform these sixteenth notes too rapidly, without giving them time to "sound." The result is an unclear rendition that is often out of tune.

GENERAL RULE: Sing fast-moving figures a bit slower than indicated if the style of the song permits, to allow shorter notes to be heard.

Measure 4: Sustain the dotted quarter notes (♩.) for their full value.
Measure 6: Sing the sixteenth notes (♪ ♪) in correct rhythm.
Measure 8: The figure ♫ ♩ ♫ is a syncopation (a displacement of normal beat or accent).

GENERAL RULE: When learning songs that have rhythmic problems, speak the words in correct rhythm before singing. If you cannot speak them in correct rhythm, you cannot sing them correctly.

Measures 9–13: The two phrases here are exactly alike; they should be sung so as to create musical contrast. Observe the dynamic markings printed over these phrases, and the desired contrast will be attained.

Along with Schubert's slow, atmospheric song, see page 196 for Michael Arne's "The Lass with the Delicate Air." Michael Arne was the son of the important eighteenth-century English composer Dr. Thomas Arne.

Sing "The Lass with the Delicate Air" gracefully and with good humor.

Wanderer's Night Song
Wanderers Nachtlied

Johann Wolfgang von Goethe

Franz Schubert

The *IH* Vowel

Webster's New World:	i
American Heritage:	ĭ
International:	I

WORDS WITH THE *IH* VOWEL

Read aloud slowly:

bid	sit	him	since
rid	mid	lift	tint
bit	miss	lit	din
kit	pit	slip	mint

Sing:

1. Very slowly.

mid	fin - ish		thing	him	lift	lit	slip
rid	lip	bid	sip	since	tint	din	mint

2. Very slowly.

mid	bid	him	lift	lit
fit	sip	since	tint	din

3. Very slowly; sing with one breath.

him _____	lift _____	lit
since _____	din _____	mint
rip _____	sit _____	big
bu - sy	ring	is

4. Moderately; sing with one breath.

bid _____	fin - ish _____	thing
him _____	lift _____	lit _____	slip
rid _____	lip _____	mid _____	sip
since _____	tint _____	din _____	mint

SENTENCES WITH THE *IH* VOWEL

Sing until all *IH* vowels are clearly executed

1. Very slowly.

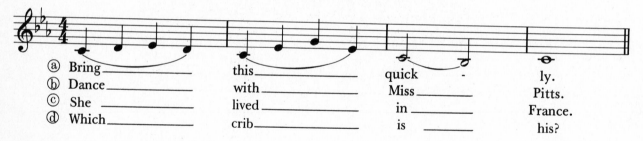

ⓐ Bring _____	this _____	quick -	ly.
ⓑ Dance _____	with _____	Miss _____	Pitts.
ⓒ She _____	lived _____	in _____	France.
ⓓ Which _____	crib _____	is _____	his?

2. Very slowly.

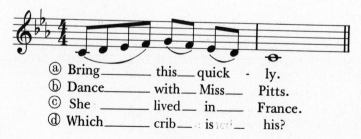

| ⓐ Bring _ | this _ | quick- | ly. _ ⓑ Dance _ | with _ | Miss _ | Pitts. _ |
| ⓒ She _ | lived _ | in _ | France. _ ⓓ Which _ | crib _ | is _ | his? _ |

3. Moderately.

ⓐ Bring _____	this _ quick -	ly.
ⓑ Dance _____	with _ Miss _	Pitts.
ⓒ She _____	lived _ in _	France.
ⓓ Which _____	crib _ is _	his?

4. Sing with one breath.

ⓐ She _____ lived   in ___ France._____
ⓑ Dance_____ with   Miss ___ Pitts. _____
ⓒ Which_____ crib   is ___ his? _____
ⓓ This_____ man   sings ___ songs._____

STUDY

The *IH* (i, ĭ) Vowel: Description and Execution

The *IH* vowel is a closed, bright, front vowel and is executed as follows:

1. The front of the tongue is raised, but not so high as for *EE*.
2. The tip of the tongue is forward.
3. The upper lip is raised in a smiling position.
4. The jaw is dropped slightly to about the same position as for *EE*. *IH* and *EE* are the only front vowels that are closed.

The *IH* (ɪ) Vowel: Common Faults and Corrections

Practice speaking and singing the following words:

d*i*vine	w*i*nd (noun)
pr*e*tty	g*i*ve
b*u*sy	w*o*men
beaut*i*ful	r*hy*thm

When singing final unstressed *y* or *ies*, sing *EE* or *EEz*. The vowel sound should not be *IH*. This applies especially when final *y* is rhymed with final *EE*, as in "love*ly*" and "th*ee*," "mystery" and "sl*ee*p," "melo*dy*" and "sh*e*." (NOTE: *y* is sometimes a diphthong, as in *my, thy*, and *sky*. See Lesson 10.)

General Principles of Singing

It was pointed out in Lesson 2 that certain vowels are called "fundamental," while others are called "subordinate" because they are considered modifications of the fundamental sounds. The vowels *EE, EH, AH, AW*, and $\overline{OO}$ are fundamental; all other vowels are subordinate.

Figure 8–1 shows the relative tongue positions for each of the front vowels, from most closed to most open. Notice that, for each vowel position, the tongue is forward and the front is raised. In the next lesson, the other vowels will be similarly diagrammed.

Good health plays an important role in fine singing. When a singer is "in good voice," this can usually be attributed to a balanced diet, proper exercise, rest, and other essentials of good health. Singers, like athletes, should have

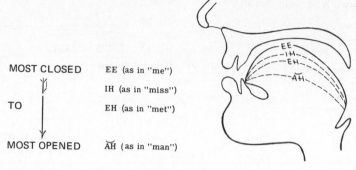

MOST CLOSED   EE (as in "me")

TO   IH (as in "miss")

               EH (as in "met")

MOST OPENED   ĂH (as in "man")

FIGURE 8–1

their own training rules. They should avoid smoking; they should get a full night's sleep each night in a well-ventilated room; they should establish a balanced diet, including vitamin supplements if necessary; and they should exercise outdoors each day, if only by taking a long, brisk walk.

Observe the following rules of vocal hygiene:

Do not abuse your voice. Yelling at sports events may reflect good school spirit, but it is deadly for the voice. Go to the games or play in them, but contribute your portion of cheer without yelling.

Make rest periods as important as practice periods. Like other parts of the body, the vocal organs and muscles require rest after use. These muscles work almost twice as much when singing as when speaking. In speaking, it is estimated that the vocal bands phonate about 45 to 50 percent of the time; in singing, about 90 to 95 percent of the time. Arrange your schedule so that you have ample rest between practice periods. Do not practice early in the morning or immediately after a heavy meal. Develop note-reading ability, so that you can learn songs by reading them over silently.

Sing carefully when you have a head cold or minor throat irritation. These conditions are not injurious to the vocal bands when the tone is produced correctly. If, however, your breathing begins to be affected, *stop singing.*

Never force the voice. Never sing louder than you can sing with a good tone. A forced tone is *always* a bad tone.

If laryngitis develops, see your physician. Do not speak or sing for the duration of the infection.

Two common results of the misuse of the voice are:

Tremolo.   Tremolo is an excessive waver in the voice which causes distortion of the desired pitch. Tremolos may be fast, resembling a goat's bleat, or slow, characterized by an undulation or wobble. Both types are undesirable; they can be corrected only by rest and proper attention to posture, breathing, and elimination of tension in the vocal muscles and organs. Tremolo should not be confused with *vibrato.* A warm, natural vibrato is the rapid iteration of one tone which is produced by the fully resonated voice. It does not distort pitch.

Vocal nodes.   Vocal nodes are tiny, hardened spots, resembling calluses, which form on the margins of the vocal bands. Continued misuse of the voice causes the nodes to become firmer, until they form a wedge between the bands. Such a condition prevents the bands from correct phonation and causes chronic hoarseness. To overcome the obstacle, the singer with nodes usually forces the voice, causing the condition to worsen. Nodes are often cured by complete rest, which permits the bands to heal (much as calluses on the hands will heal). Nodes seldom develop when singers take good care of their voices and use them correctly. However, if nodes do develop, one is faced with a *medical,* not a *musical,* problem, and a laryngologist should be consulted immediately.

The larynx, which houses the vocal bands, is one of the most marvelous instruments in the body. It deserves good care, for it has many functions. First, it is an important part of the respiratory system, acting as a passageway for the ingress and egress of air. Second, it functions as a protective valve for the respiratory tract by keeping foreign matter out. (If you have ever had food or water "go down the wrong way," you know how important the larynx is, both in keeping foreign matter out and in coughing it up when it does enter.) Finally, the larynx, acting as a valve, closes the air passageway, trapping air in the lungs to prepare the thorax for bodily effort. Those who have had their larynxes removed lose the ability to speak normally and find it difficult to lift heavy objects, blow their noses, or blow out a match, and they lose much of their sense of smell.

The larynx is shown in Figure 8–2.

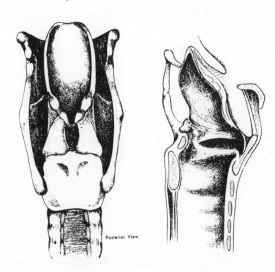

Posterior View

FIGURE 8–2
Larynx; Interior of Larynx

SONG INTERPRETATION AND MUSICIANSHIP
Handel, "Where'er You Walk"

This song should be sung lyrically, with deep feeling. Though it is a love song, do not sing it in the style of popular love songs. There should be a feeling of dignity and stateliness.

Memorize the following:

D.C. al Fine: D.C. *(da capo)* means "from the beginning"; *al Fine* means "to the word *Fine (end).*"

Adagio: slow. In the music of the eighteenth century, *adagio* is often used to indicate a temporary change to a slower tempo, as at cadences.

Measure 2: Do not sing the 32nd-notes (♪♬) as sixteenth notes (♩♬). Although these notes move rapidly, give them time to be heard.

Measures 12–13: These are to be sung with one breath. The rests are observed by stopping the sound but not by taking a new breath.

Measures 14–15: The rests in measure 15 help to prepare the slower tempo. Make a slight *ritard* in measure 14, giving the quarter note on "sit" a bit more than its full value; then, after a pause, sing the notes in measure 15 with a feeling of cadence.

At the time when Handel wrote his music, singers embellished songs as much as they desired. Composers allowed for this individuality by putting in long pauses, cadences, and indications where a cadenza would be most appropriate. Therefore, when singing this composition, mold your phrases and sing with a florid style, adding ornamentation such as trills and appoggiaturas where appropriate. Invent a cadenza in measure 26 and a more florid one in measure 16 after the repeat.

The text of this song and fragments of the text are repeated with contrasting embellishments and florid treatment. It is this florid, irregular treatment which caused the name *Baroque* (meaning literally "irregular" or "grotesque") to be given to the period in which this music was written.

Two important stylistic characteristics of Baroque music should be mentioned here.

1. *Upbeat phrasing.* The Greek word *anacrusis*, which means *upbeat,* is often used to denote this kind of phrasing. It implies that phrasing is to be across the beat and across the bar. Some examples will serve to illustrate:

a.) 1. Upbeat Phrasing

2. Beat Phrasing

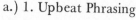

Note that, in the first example, the fourth beat is phrased across the bar to the first beat, and then the second, third, and fourth beats lead again across the bar to the next downbeat. In the second example, stresses are on the first and third beats (like a march). These accents destroy any feel of upbeat phrasing.

b.) 1.

2.

Here in the first example, the sixteenth notes are phrased so that the fourth in each group goes across the *beat* to the next group. In the second, stress is on the first sixteenth in each group of four; they are thus phrased *on* the beat, not *across* it.

c.) 1.

2.

Here again, in the first example the triplets are phrased across the beat and across the bar; in the second they are phrased *on* the beat.

These examples are a simplification of an important Baroque stylistic principle. Not only are notes within measures phrased in this manner, but entire measures often serve as upbeats to other measures and entire phrases as upbeats to other phrases. Sing each example on a neutral syllable until you feel the upbeat.

In Handel's "Where'er You Walk," phrasing has been indicated above the voice line as follows: broken lines (.⌒⁻⁻⁻⁻⌒.) indicate small phrases, boldface lines (⌒‾‾‾‾‾) indicate larger phrases. Follow this phrasing but avoid exaggeration. The great Baroque composers (Handel, Bach, Vivaldi, among others) built the style into their music—you have only to bring it out.

2. *The Doctrine of the Affections.* Baroque composers were concerned with the passions and affections, the deep-lying forces that affected emotional life. They realized that emotions were especially responsive to music. The doctrine of affections related principally to the union of music and text. Baroque composers developed a superb compositional technique known as *tone painting,* in which the music graphically mirrored the text. Ideas of movement and direction (stepping, leaping, ascending, descending) and emotional states (weeping, laughing, pleading) were represented vividly through the manipulation of melody and rhythm. Musical notes not only sounded like the affect being created; they often were made to *look* like it. A good example is the opening tenor aria in Handel's *Messiah.* After the recitative "Comfort Ye," the tenor sings, "Every valley shall be exalted, the crooked [made] straight, and the rough places plain, and every mountain and hill made low." But look what Handel does with the notes!

On the word "exalted" Handel has written an ascending sequence, thus lifting, raising, "exalting" the word both to the eye and to the ear.

1.

He builds a "mountain" with notes, then a smaller "hill," then expresses the word "low" with a low note.

2.

On the word "crooked" the note pattern is crooked, followed by a sustained, "straight" pitch.

3.

Finally he smoothes out the rough places and makes them plain.

4.

Always be sensitive to tone painting in Baroque and other music.

Another Baroque song which may be studied along with "Where'er You Walk" is "Dido's Lament" by Henry Purcell (p. 201). Purcell was an earlier Baroque composer (1659–1695) who wrote one of the truly great English operatic masterworks, *Dido and Aeneas,* from which this aria is taken. Study its Baroque characteristics. Notice how the piano introduction descends in gloomy half-steps for a full octave. The minor key is likewise appropriate for a lament. Phrase "Dido's Lament" according to the Baroque principles that have been discussed.

This aria is from *Semele,* one of the many operas written by Handel.

Where'er You Walk

George Frideric Handel

Where e'er you walk, cool gales shall fan the glade; Trees where you sit, shall crowd in - to a shade, Trees where you sit shall crowd in -

to— a shade.

Where e'er you tread, the blush-ing flow'r shall rise, And all things flour-ish, and all things flour-ish where e'er you turn your eyes, where e'er you turn your eyes, where e'er you turn your eyes.

LESSON 9

The *UH* and *OO* Vowels

Webster's New World:	u and oo
American Heritage:	ŭ and o͝o
International:	ʌ and ʊ

WORDS WITH THE *UH* AND *OO* VOWELS

Read aloud slowly:

done	fun	brook	good
hunt	sung	book	look
run	shun	took	full
sun	young	shook	would

Sing:

1. Very slowly.

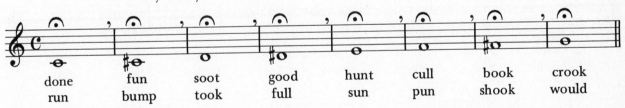

done	fun	soot	good	hunt	cull	book	crook
run	bump	took	full	sun	pun	shook	would

2. Very slowly.

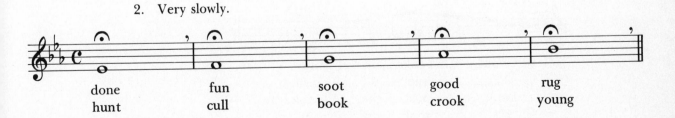

done	fun	soot	good	rug
hunt	cull	book	crook	young

3. Very slowly; sing with one breath.

done_____	hunt_____	run
sun_____	bug_____	rug
soot_____	book_____	took
shook_____	wolf_____	look

4. Moderately; sing with one breath.

done _____	fun _____	soot _____	good
hunt _____	cull _____	book _____	crook
run _____	bump _____	took _____	full
sun _____	pun _____	shook _____	would

SENTENCES WITH THE *UH* AND *ŎŎ* VOWELS

Sing until all *UH* and *ŎŎ* vowels are clearly executed.

1. Very slowly.

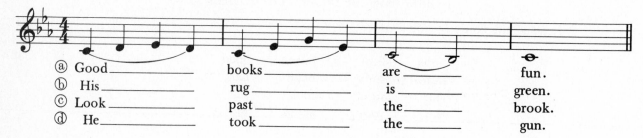

ⓐ	Good_____	books_____	are _____	fun.
ⓑ	His_____	rug_____	is _____	green.
ⓒ	Look_____	past_____	the_____	brook.
ⓓ	He_____	took_____	the_____	gun.

2. Very slowly.

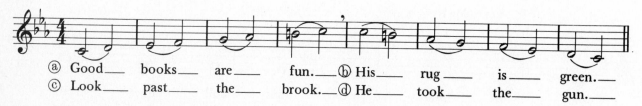

ⓐ Good__	books__	are__	fun.	ⓑ His__	rug __	is __	green.__
ⓒ Look__	past__	the__	brook.	ⓓ He__	took__	the__	gun.__

3. Moderately.

ⓐ	Good_____	books_are_____	fun.	
ⓑ	His_____	rug_	is_	green.
ⓒ	Look_____	past_	the_	brook.
ⓓ	He_____	took_	the_	gun.

4. Sing with one breath.

ⓐ	Good _____	books	are ___	fun. _____	
ⓑ	His _____	rug	is ___	green. _____	
ⓒ	Look _____	past	the ___	brook. _____	
ⓓ	He _____	took	the ___	gun. _____	

STUDY

The *UH* (u, ŭ) and *OŎ* (oo, ŏŏ) Vowels: Description and Execution

The *UH* vowel is open. *UH*, a modification of fundamental *AH*, is similar in quality and execution, but the tongue is in a slightly different position and the jaw is not so low. Sing *UH* as follows:

1. The middle of the tongue is raised slightly.
2. The tip of the tongue is forward.
3. The lips are in a relaxed, neutral position.
4. The jaw is dropped in a relaxed position.

The *OŎ* vowel is an open vowel and is a modification of fundamental $\overline{OO}$ (*lose*). It is sometimes called "medial" to denote its place between $\overline{OO}$ and *AW*. *OŎ* is sung as follows:

1. The middle of the tongue is raised higher than for *UH*.
2. The tip of the tongue is forward.
3. The lips are slightly rounded and protruded, but must be relaxed.
4. The jaw is dropped in a relaxed position.

The *UH* (ʌ) and *OŎ* (ʊ) Vowels: Common Faults and Corrections

The *UH* vowel is usually easy to sing. It appears infrequently and should never be sung except when appropriate, since too much use of this sound thickens and deadens the resonance of the voice. Clear execution of *UH* is often important. For example, in the prefix *un-*, *UH* must be distinct, since *un-* is a syllable that changes or denies the meaning of the word to which it is joined. Practice speaking and singing the following words:

unwise   unknown   unkind   unsung

The rounding of the lips when singing *OŎ* is greater than when singing $\overline{OO}$. If the rounding is too slight, the sense of many words may be changed: *look* becomes *Luke*, *full* becomes *fool*, and *soot* becomes *suit*. Practice until you can make a clear distinction between these sounds.

General Principles of Singing

With the conclusion of the present lesson, nine front, middle, and back vowels have been studied. Figure 9–1 shows the positions of the middle and back vowels. The tip of the tongue remains forward for each of these vowels, and the back or middle of the tongue is raised.

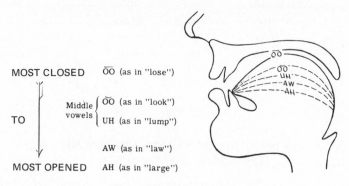

MOST CLOSED   OO (as in "lose")

TO   Middle vowels { OO (as in "look")
                      UH (as in "lump")

                     AW (as in "law")
MOST OPENED   AH (as in "large")

FIGURE 9–1

Two other vowel sounds remain to be studied:

1. *The weak vowel* (ə).   This vowel sound, which appears only in unstressed syllables, derives its name from its short, indefinite character. In each of the following words, a syllable with the weak vowel is in italics.

*o*cean	hand*some*	*na*tion	com*fort*
glad*ness*	trea*sure*	sad*ness*	*the* (before a consonant sound)
nev*er*	need*ed*	*of*	*a* (before a consonant sound)

The weak vowel appears so frequently in English that it is impossible to list all of its forms. Moreover, this vowel cannot be practiced as a separate, distinct sound detached from a word, but rather must be practiced only in context. It must be executed with exactly the right duration and quality; if it is stressed or unduly prolonged, diction sounds distorted and affected.[1] Thus, "heede*d*" becomes "he-*dead*," "*of*" becomes "*awv*," and "*the* boy" becomes "*thah* boy." Recognize this sound wherever it appears and produce it properly.

2. *The umlaut vowel* (IPA: з).   Although spelled in various ways, the umlaut vowel is always followed by the consonant *r*.

b*ir*d	b*ur*n	w*or*d	t*ur*n	h*er*
l*ear*n	f*ir*m	y*ear*n	st*ir*	g*ir*l

This sound is called the umlaut vowel because it sounds almost the same as the German *o* with umlaut *(ö)*. (The word *umlaut* means "change the sound.") As you can see, the vowel sound has many spellings in English.

Sing the umlaut vowel with the lips curled forward like the bell of a horn. Retain this position up and down the scale, lowering the jaw as the voice goes higher. Soften *r* before a consonant sound. (See Lesson 16.)

---

1. Exceptions occur only when a composer has placed a syllable with the weak vowel on a sustained note.

SONG INTERPRETATION AND MUSICIANSHIP
Grieg, "Boat Song" ("Im Kahne")

The tempo is marked *allegretto grazioso*, which means "with some animation" (*allegretto*) "in a graceful style" (*grazioso*).

Measures 5–10: Execute the chord intervals without sliding from one note to another. The octave skip from measure 6 to 7 may be particularly awkward. Octaves are difficult to sing, and should be practiced up and down the scale.

Measures 13–15: The descending chromatic passages sometimes present problems because of the tendency to descend too much in the descending intervals.

GENERAL RULE: When singing descending intervals, think of the interval as being smaller and closer to the one above. In ascending passages, think of the interval as being larger.

Measure 17: The key changes to E major. This is called a *modulation*.

Measures 17–22: Practice the expanding intervals as a separate exercise. Measures 17–18 have a skip of a third; 19–20, a skip of a fourth; 21, a skip of a fifth. To prepare for these intervals, practice the following exercise in various keys, singing neutral syllables or a single vowel.

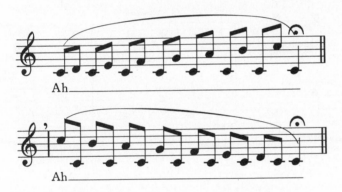

Measures 23–25: There is a modulation back to F major. Double dots at double bar lines ‖: :‖ indicate that music in between is to be repeated. The first ending [1. 2.] is sung at the end of all stanzas except the last; for the last stanza, the second ending is used.

See Roger Quilter's "O Mistress Mine" on p. 204, another song requiring a graceful, controlled style of singing. Quilter was an English composer known chiefly for his songs, most of which are graceful settings of English lyrics, many by Shakespeare. This song is in strophic form. Sing it with warmth and tenderness.

Grieg's songs owe much of their popularity to the piquant and expressive melodic idioms which he borrowed from the folksongs of Norway. His "Boat Song" is inimitable in its charm and delicacy.

Boat Song
Im Kahne

Allegretto grazioso

Edvard Grieg
(1843—1907)

1. Sea - gulls, sea - gulls a - bove are flock - ing in bright sun - shine;
2. Loos - en, loos - en, my love, thy hood o'er tress - es bright;
3. Rock me rock me, O gen - tle rip - plets from the sea;

Each lit - tle gos - ling with yel - low stock - ings clear and fine;
Then we will dance in the warm and shin - ing moon-lit night;
Fair my__ love, as a young fawn slend - er, comes to me;

Row, row, to Fish - er's strand, all is calm as we
Wait! wait! we must de - lay, There'll be danc - ing on
Rock, rock in dreams di - vine, I am thine and__

near the land, Seas are ly - ing so still, Oh!
wed - ding day, Fid - dles play - ing their fill, Oh!
thou art mine, Vi - o - lins now are still, Oh!

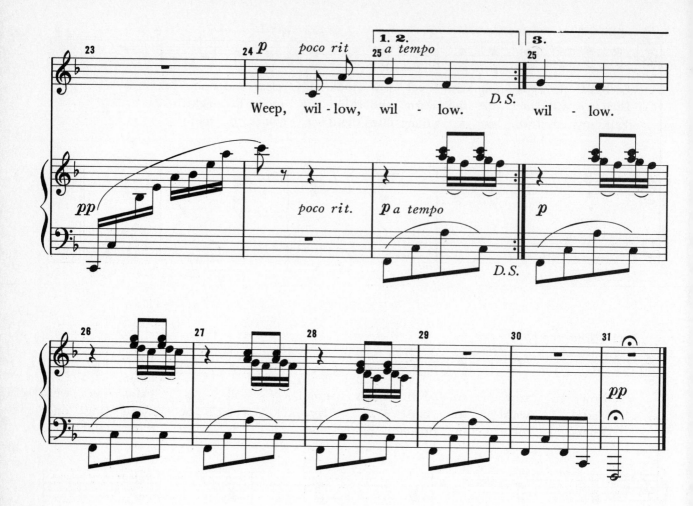

Weep, wil - low, wil - low. wil - low.

LESSON 10

The *EH-IH*, *OH-OO*, and *AH-IH* Diphthongs

Webster's New World:	ā, ō, and ī
American Heritage:	ā, ō, and ī
International:	ɛɪ, oʊ, and aɪ

WORDS WITH THE *EH-IH*, *OH-OO*, AND *AH-IH* DIPHTHONGS

Read aloud slowly:

may	say	oh	blow	I	might
pay	praise	no	row	my	ride
play	aid	snow	throw	why	chime
lay	day	so	flow	die	find

Sing:

1. Very slowly.

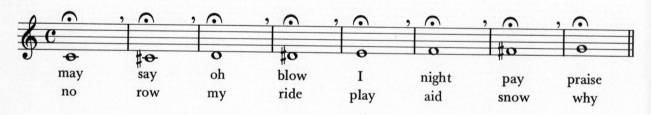

may	say	oh	blow	I	night	pay	praise
no	row	my	ride	play	aid	snow	why

2. Very slowly.

throw	chime	lay	day	so
flow	die	find	may	oh

90

3. Very slowly; sing with one breath.

may_____	say_____	pay
no_____	oh _____	throw
night_____	my_____	I
lay_____	throw_____	why

4. Moderately; sing with one breath.

may_____	say_____	pay _____	praise
no_____	oh_____	row_____	snow
my_____	night_____	I _____	why
lay_____	flow_____	find _____	day

SENTENCES WITH THE *EH-IH, OH-OO,* AND *AH-IH* DIPHTHONGS

Sing until all diphthongs are clearly executed.

1. Very slowly.

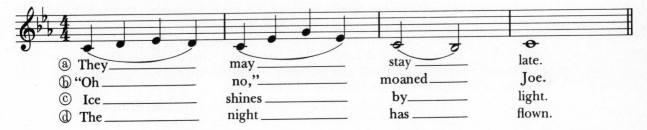

ⓐ They_____	may_____	stay _____	late.
ⓑ "Oh_____	no," _____	moaned_____	Joe.
ⓒ Ice_____	shines _____	by_____	light.
ⓓ The_____	night_____	has _____	flown.

2. Very slowly.

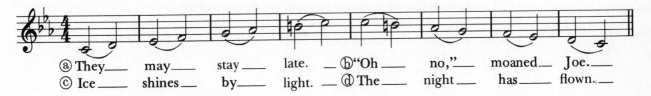

| ⓐ They___ | may___ | stay___ | late. ___ | ⓑ"Oh ___ | no," ___ | moaned___ | Joe. ___ |
| ⓒ Ice ___ | shines___ | by___ | light. ___ | ⓓ The ___ | night ___ | has ___ | flown. |

3. Moderately.

ⓐ They_____	may___	stay ___	late.
ⓑ "Oh_____	no," ___	moaned	Joe.
ⓒ Ice_____	shines___	by___	light.
ⓓ The_____	night ___	has ___	flown.

4. Sing with one breath.

a They_____ may stay__ late s_____
b "Oh_____ no," moaned Joe._____
c Ice_____ shines by__ light_____
d The_____ night has__ flown._____

STUDY

The EH-IH (ā), OH-OO (ō), and AH-IH (ī) Diphthongs: Description and Execution

A diphthong is a syllable which combines two vowel sounds. The word *diph-thong* (pronounced "dihf-thawng") is derived from the Greek *di-* (meaning *twice*) and *phthongos* (meaning *sounds*). In all diphthongs, one of the vowel sounds is stressed and sustained; the other is unstressed and short. The two vowel sounds are referred to as (1) the sustained sound, and (2) the vanishing sound.

The diphthong *EH-IH* combines two front, bright vowel sounds. *EH (met)* is the sustained sound; *IH (miss)* is the vanishing sound. Refer to Lesson 3 for a description of *EH* and to Lesson 8 for *IH*.

The diphthong *OH-OO* combines two back, dark vowel sounds. *OH (obey)* is the sustained sound; *OO (look)* is the vanishing sound. *OH* is a pure sound (IPA: o) *only* in words in which it is unstressed. For example, *OH* is pure in "*o*bey," "*o*vert," "p*o*lite," and "mem*o*ry." When *OH* is pure, it is always spelled *o*. *OH* is diphthongized in all words and exclamations of one syllable (*oh, no, cold, rose*) and in all words of more than one syllable within which it receives any stress (*only, devotion, motion*). When diphthongized, *OH* is combined with *OO* (*look*). *OH* is sung the same way, whether it is pure or the first part of a diphthong:

1. The back of the tongue is raised higher than for *AW*.
2. The tip of the tongue is forward.
3. The lips are allowed to purse farther forward than for *AW*, forming an oval shape.
4. The jaw is down in a relaxed position.

Do not tense the lips, since this will result in a "tight" tone. Allow the lips to round, but keep the rounding comparatively large. Do not protrude them too much.

In some sections of the United States, *OH* is attacked with an *EH* sound, followed by a glide into pure *OH*. Thus, *go* becomes *geh⁀o* and *blow* becomes *bleh⁀o*. To avoid this, shape the lips for *OH* before rather than after the attack.

The diphthong *AH-IH* combines one dark, back vowel sound and one front, bright vowel sound. *AH (as in farm)* is the sustained sound: *IH (as in miss)* is the vanishing sound. (Refer to Lesson 4 for *AH* and to Lesson 8 for *IH*.)

The *EH-IH*(ɛɪ), *OH-OŎ*(ou), and *AH-IH*(aɪ) Diphthongs: Common Faults and Corrections

Avoid distorting either vowel sound in a diphthong. Some singers are oblivious to this fault until corrected; they sing *geh-oh* for *go*, or *toh-ihm* for *time*. Understand the form of the diphthong and avoid this mistake.

Do not omit the second sound in a diphthong. It must be articulated clearly if the word is to be understood.

An important principle about diphthongs is that only one of the vowel sounds is sustained and stressed. Do not copy the diction of popular singers, who often distort the time values of diphthongs in order to achieve an effect of intimacy, a technique which is acceptable only for popular music.

The following shows the relative time values for each of the two vowel sounds in the word *night:*

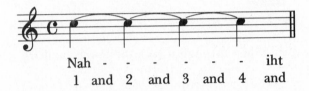

The *AH* sound is sustained until after the fourth count, at which time *IH*, the vanishing sound, is briefly articulated.

Do not change the second vowel sound in *EH-IH* to *EE*. When this is done, *grace* sounds like *grease*, *may* like *me*, and *say* like *see*. Sing *IH* clearly.

Stressed *o* is pronounced as a diphthong. Some students pronounce only the *AW*, omitting the second sound *(OŎ)* entirely; they sing "*Gaw* 'way from my wind*aw*" and "*Law* how a r*aw*z. . . ." Learn to recognize both of the vowel sounds in a diphthong, and pronounce each correctly.

SONG INTERPRETATION AND MUSICIANSHIP

Brahms, "Sapphic Ode" ("Sapphische Ode")

This song should be sung slowly but with movement. Do not drag. The syncopated accompaniment provides underlying movement. The term *mezzo voce* means to use only half *(mezzo)* the power of the voice *(voce)*.

When studying the diphthongs in this work, first isolate the sounds by circling the words containing them. Underneath these diphthongs, write lightly in pencil the sustained sound in capital letters and the vanishing sound in small letters; for example:

```
"Ro - ses      I          at      night"
ROH-oo         AH-ih              NAH-ih
```

The sustained sound is thereby highlighted.

Review the songs covered in previous lessons, looking for the three diphthongs presented in this lesson. As other diphthongs are introduced, restudy all the earlier songs in similar fashion.

This song has changes of measure length. Retain the half note as the unit of beat throughout. Note how the double bar (‖) indicates that a change is to occur.

See also Franz Schubert's "Ave Maria" on page 207. The style of "Ave Maria" is legato. It should be sung with reverence and deep religious feeling, but do not overemotionalize or sentimentalize.

Memorize the following:

pp (pianissimo): very softly

> (rinforzando): accented

dim. (diminuendo): gradually diminishing in volume

~ *(mordent):* a group of two or more grace notes played or sung rapidly before a principal note, consisting of the principal note itself and the note above it. The mordent in measure 11 would be written out as follows:

If the same sign is used with a vertical line through it (**~**), the lower auxiliary note is sung:

The training text of "Ave Maria" is made up almost entirely of words with the *EH-IH* sound.

Measures 1–2: The piano has a harplike pattern. These notes should be played so that the rise and fall of the chordal pattern is gently curved. The left-hand octaves should not be thumped.

Measure 4: Sing the grace notes delicately. Practice them as a separate exercise until you are able to sing them with agility.

Measures 6–7: Do not slur the triplets so that there is a loss of pitch definition. Strive for clear, sharply defined movement between these notes, but do not lose the legato style. Do not sing with the aspirate in order to achieve clarity. Practice these triplets as a separate exercise.

Measure 7: Take a "catch breath" after the first *thee.*

Measure 8: Practice the grace-note figure as an exercise for clarity and flexibility.

GENERAL RULE: When learning a melody to which grace notes have been added, first practice the main melody notes without ornamentation. When these notes are secure, add the grace notes without disturbing the rhythmic flow. Do not sing them too rapidly—give them time to sound. In music composed after 1800, the grace note is usually sung slightly before the beat.

Measure 11: Practice the inverted mordent as a separate exercise until you can sing it smoothly.

The small note ⚬ is called an *appoggiatura. Appoggiatura* is taken from the Italian word *appoggiare* meaning "to lean." It is one of the most charming embellishments of song, and often has a yearning, sorrowful, or tender character. The appoggiatura is almost always extraneous to the harmony with which it appears. Before an undotted note, it generally receives its face value—that is, one-half the value of the note which follows. Before a dotted note, it usually receives more than its face value—that is, about two-thirds the value of the following note. In performance, the appoggiatura always receives the accent. If there is a diagonal line through the small note, ♪ , it is called an *acciaccatura* and is sung twice as rapidly. (*Acciaccatura* means "crushed," and refers to the way the notes seem to be squeezed together.)

Appoggiaturas in this song, as in most music before 1800, should be sung *on* the beat.

Measure 12: The appoggiatura appears again.

Although students are urged to begin with the training text, the Latin text should also be learned and sung. Liturgical (church) Latin employs basically only five vowel sounds, which are easy to learn: *AH, EH, EE, AW, OO.* Here is the text of the "Ave Maria" spelled phonetically; stressed syllables are in capital letters.

Stanza I
AH-veh mah-REE-ah, GRAH-tsee-ah PLEH-nah,
DAW-mee-noos TEH-koom,
beh-neh-DEEK-tah TOO een moo-lee-EH-ree-boos,
eht beh-neh-DEEK-toos FROOK-toos VEHN-trees TOO-ee YEH-soos.

Stanza II
AH-veh mah-REE-ah, MAH-tehr DEH-ee,
AW-rah praw NAW-bees peh-cah-TAW-ree-boos,
NOONK eht een AW-rah MAWR-tees NAW-streh.

Another song with many diphthongs is Edward Purcell's "Passing By," which you will find on page 212. Edward Purcell was the brother of Henry Purcell. This song, in strophic form, should be sung quite simply but with expression. Note that the first verse seeks to tell the audience a story; the second verse is more intimate; the third is declamatory. Following a four-bar introduction, the song is sixteen bars long. You should feel the melody in four-bar phrases, but make each phrase relate to the next so that all sixteen bars unfold as a unified melody.

There are hardly any singers today who do not include some songs of Brahms in their repertory. As was pointed out in Lesson 4, many of Brahms's songs are based on German folk songs which he collected and edited.

Sapphic Ode[1]
Sapphische Ode

German text by
Hans Schmidt

Johannes Brahms
(1833–1897)

Rather slowly

1. Training text: Ro - ses I at night from the hedge - rows
2. German text: Ro - sen brach ich nachts mir am dunk - len

p mezza voce

sev - ered, Sweet - er was their scent than in day - time
Ha - ge; süs - ser hauch - ten Duft sie, als je am

ev - er; Yet the trem - bling branch - es so soft - ly
Ta - ge, doch ver - streu - ten reich die be - weg - ten

pp

----

1. Sapphic refers to Sappho, the ancient Greek poet famous for her love lyrics.

night from thy lips—— I've ta - ken:
Strauch dei -ner Lip - pen pflück - te:

Yet thou
doch auch

too were trem -bling and soft - ly   mov - ing,   Tear - - drops be -
dir, be -wegt im Ge -müth gleich je - nen,   thau - - ten die

dewed———————— thee.
Thrä - - nen.

The AH͡-UH, AW͡-IH, and IH͡-OO Diphthongs

Webster's New World:	ou, oi, and yo͞o
American Heritage:	ou, oi, and yo͞o
International:	aʊ, ɔī, and ɪu

WORDS WITH THE AH͡-UH, AW͡-IH, AND IH͡-OO DIPHTHONGS

Read aloud slowly:

vow	out	voice	choice	view	new
brown	round	poise	Roy	due	mute
how	bow	noise	boy	few	pew
shout	now	joy	toy	cute	hue

Sing:

1. Very slowly.

now	brown	how	shout	out	round	bow	vow
noise	voice	poise	joy	choice	Roy	boy	toy
new	view	due	few	cute	mute	pew	hue

2. Very slowly.

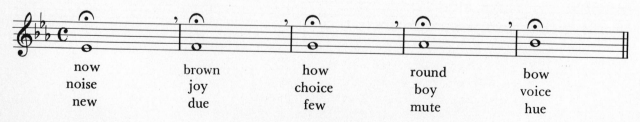

now	brown	how	round	bow
noise	joy	choice	boy	voice
new	due	few	mute	hue

3. Very slowly; sing with one breath.

now	how	round
noise	joy	boy
new	few	mute
bow	voice	due

4. Moderately; sing with one breath.

now	how	round	bow
noise	joy	boy	voice
new	few	mute	due
vow	poise	view	out

SENTENCES WITH AH-UH, AW-IH, AND IH-OO DIPHTHONGS

Sing until all diphthongs are clearly executed.

1. Very slowly.

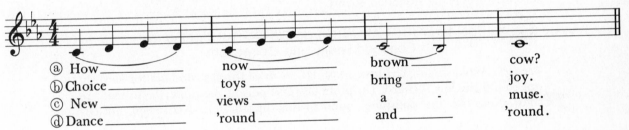

ⓐ How_____ now_____ brown_____ cow?
ⓑ Choice_____ toys_____ bring _____ joy.
ⓒ New_____ views_____ a - muse.
ⓓ Dance_____ 'round_____ and_____ 'round.

2. Very slowly.

ⓐ How___ now___ brown___ cow?___ ⓑ Choice___ toys___ bring___ joy.___
ⓒ New___ views___ a - muse.___ ⓓ Dance___'round___ and___ 'round.___

3. Moderately.

ⓐ How_____ now___brown___ cow?
ⓑ Choice_____ toys___ bring___ joy.
ⓒ New_____views___ a - muse.
ⓓ Dance_____ 'round___ and ___ 'round.

4. Sing with one breath.

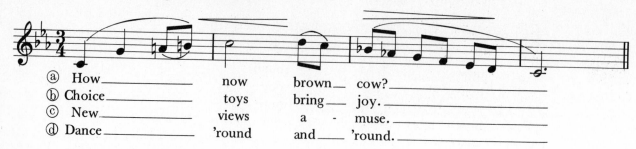

ⓐ How_____   now   brown___ cow?_____
ⓑ Choice_____   toys   bring___ joy. _____
ⓒ New_____   views   a - muse. _____
ⓓ Dance_____   'round   and___ 'round. _____

STUDY

The *AH͡-UH* (ou), *AW͡-IH* (oi), and *IH͡-OO* (iu) Diphthongs: Description and Execution

The diphthong *AH͡-UH* combines one back, dark vowel and one middle vowel. *AH (large)* is the sustained sound; *UH (lump)* is the vanishing sound. (Refer to Lesson 4 for a description of *AH*, and to Lesson 9 for *UH*.)

The diphthong *AW͡-IH* combines one back vowel and one front vowel. *AW (call)* is the sustained vowel; *IH (miss)* is the vanishing vowel. (Refer to Lesson 6 for a description of *AW*, and to Lesson 8 for *IH*.)

The diphthong *IH͡-OO* combines one front vowel and one back vowel. *IH (miss)* is the vanishing sound; *OO (lose)* is the sustained sound. (Refer to Lesson 8 for *IH* and to Lesson 7 for *OO*.) *IH͡-OO* is the only diphthong in which the second vowel is the sustained sound.

The *AH͡-UH* (aʊ), *AW͡-IH* (ɔɪ), and *IH͡-OO* (Iu) Diphthongs: Common Faults and Corrections

AH͡-UH: Avoid singing *OH* instead of *AH*, as in *no* for *now*, and *hoe* for *how*. Do not round the lips forward. Drop the jaw and permit the upper front teeth to show. Note that the vanishing sound in this diphthong is *UH (lump)*, not *OO (move)*.

AW͡-IH: Avoid singing *AH* for *AW* in this diphthong. Round the lips forward in an oval shape; otherwise you will sing *buy* for *boy*, and *tie* for *toy*. Do not omit the second vowel; otherwise *poise* becomes *paws*, and *joy* becomes *jaw*.

IH͡-OO: Articulate the first vowel, or *due* will sound like *do*, and *mute* like *moot*. Sing the sustained sound as *OO (move)*, not *OO (look)*.

Singing diphthongs requires moving from one vowel position to another. The change must be made smoothly in a kind of "tonal glide." This movement must take place without any break in the tonal line, even when moving from a dark to a bright vowel, or from a front to a back vowel. Avoid vocal tension by relaxing the throat, tongue, jaw, and lips. Support and energize tones by correct breathing and breath control.

SONG INTERPRETATION AND MUSICIANSHIP

Folk song, "Bendemeer's Stream"

Sing in a graceful, lyrical fashion, avoiding heaviness. The words are narrative; seek to tell a story.

The abbreviation *ten,* for *tenuto,* means "held"—that is, to be sustained beyond full value.

One of the difficulties in singing a song of this type is to retain its folklike simplicity while maintaining interest. Overblown dramatics or excessive rubato are incorrect—all effects must be subtle.

Like most folk songs, this song is strophic. Because there is no harmonic or melodic difference from verse to verse, strophic settings are difficult to perform expressively. Performance requires imagination and subtle variety.

On page 216 may be found a song written for this book by the American composer Wallace DePue. "Little Lamb," a setting of a poem by William Blake, should be sung simply and reflectively. Dr. DePue is a professor of composition in the College of Musical Arts at Bowling Green State University.

This famous folk song tells of the beauties of nature by Bendemeer's Stream.

Bendemeer's Stream

Irish Folk Song

Thomas Moore
(1779–1852)

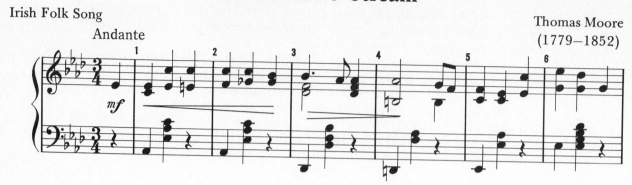

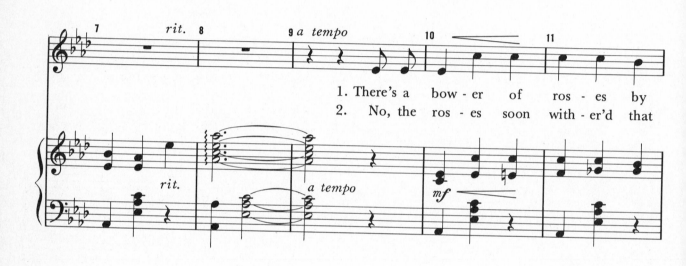

1. There's a bow - er of ros - es by
2. No, the ros - es soon with - er'd that

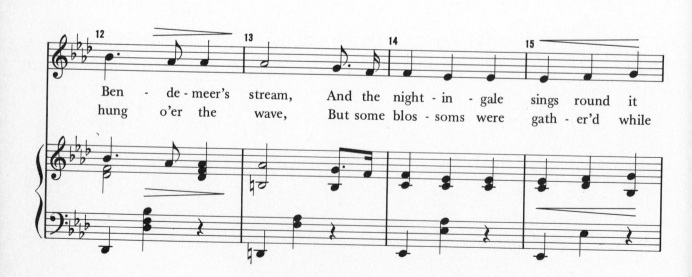

Ben - de - meer's stream, And the night - in - gale sings round it
hung o'er the wave, But some blos - soms were gath - er'd while

all   the day   long.   In the   time of   my   child - hood 'twas
fresh - ly they   shone.   And a   dew was   dis - till'd from their

like a sweet   dream,   To   sit in the   ros - es   and
flow - ers that   gave   All the   fra - grance of   sum - mer when

hear   the bird's   song.   That   bow'r and its   mus - ic   I
sum - mer was   gone.   Thus   mem - o - ry   draws from   de -

never for-get, But oft when a-lone in the bloom of the
light e'er it dies, An es-sence that breathes of it man-y a

year, I think: "Is the night-in-gale sing-ing there
year, Thus joy to my soul, as 'twas then to my

yet? Are the ros-es still bright by the calm Ben-de-meer?"
eyes, Is that bow'r on the banks of the calm Ben-de-meer.

LESSON 12

The *FAIR*, *FEAR*, and *FOUR* Diphthongs

Webster's New World:	er, ir, and ôr
American Heritage:	âr, îr, and r
International:	ɛə, ɪə, and ɔə

WORDS WITH THE *FAIR*, *FEAR*, AND *FOUR* DIPHTHONGS

Read aloud slowly:

air	dare	here	dear	more	sore
fair	care	fear	near	roar	door
chair	pair	clear	bier	floor	o'er
there	hair	pier	cheer	pore	shore

Sing:

1. Very slowly.

air	fair	chair	there	dare	care	pair	hair
here	fear	clear	pier	dear	near	bier	cheer
more	roar	floor	pore	sore	door	o'er	shore

2. Very slowly.

air	fair	chair	there	dare
here	fear	clear	pier	dear
more	roar	floor	pore	sore

3. Very slowly; sing with one breath.

air	fair	chair
here	fear	near
more	floor	shore
care	cheer	sore

4. Moderately; sing with one breath.

fair _____	chair_____	dare _____	care
here _____	fear _____	near _____	cheer
more_____	floor _____	shore _____	o'er
care _____	bier _____	sore _____	air

SENTENCES WITH THE *FAIR, FEAR,* AND *FOUR* DIPHTHONGS

Sing until all diphthongs are clearly executed.

1. Very slowly.

ⓐ	Her _____	hair _____	is _____	fair.
ⓑ	Near _____	here _____	is the_____	pier.
ⓒ	Four _____	more _____	goals _____	score.
ⓓ	Their_____	cheer-_____	lead-ers _____	roar.

2. Very slowly.

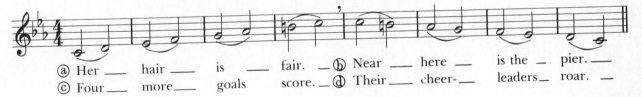

ⓐ Her __ hair __ is __ fair.		ⓑ Near __ here __	is the __ pier.__	
ⓒ Four__ more__ goals	score.__	ⓓ Their__ cheer-__	leaders_ roar. __	

3. Moderately.

ⓐ	Her	hair	is	fair.
ⓑ	Near	here	is the	pier.
ⓒ	Four	more	goals	score.
ⓓ	Their	cheer-	lead-ers	roar.

4. Sing with one breath.

ⓐ	Her _____	hair	is	fair. _____
ⓑ	Near _____	here	is the	pier. _____
ⓒ	Four _____	more	goals	score. _____
ⓓ	Their _____	cheer-	lead-ers	roar. _____

STUDY

The *FAIR* (er, âr), *FEAR* (ir, îr), and *FOUR* (ôr, r) Diphthongs: Description and Execution

Each of these diphthongs ends with the weak vowel ə, and each is always spelled with final *r* or *re*. The weak vowel is sounded in place of the final *r* or *re*.

The *FAIR* diphthong combines one front, bright vowel with the weak vowel. *EH (met)* is the sustained sound.

The *FEAR* diphthong combines one front, bright vowel with the weak vowel. *IH (miss)* is the sustained sound.

The *FOUR* diphthong combines one dark, back vowel with the weak vowel. *AW (paw)* is the sustained sound.

The *FAIR* (ɛə), *FEAR* (ɪə), and *FOUR* (ɔə) Diphthongs: Common Faults and Corrections

FAIR (ɛə): Sing the *EH* (ɛ) vowel without undue tension in the lips. Avoid any accent in the change to the weak vowel; make the change as smoothly as possible, keeping the second vowel weak. Do not substitute *AH* or *UH*. When *FAIR* is followed by a syllable or word beginning with a vowel, an *r* is added to the diphthong.[1] When an *r* is added, make certain the diphthong is clearly executed.

FEAR (ɪə): Do not substitute *EE* (i) for *IH* (ɪ). Make the change from *IH* to the weak vowel as smooth as possible. Add *r* before a vowel sound.

FOUR (ɔə): The following words should be pronounced so as to rhyme with *poor*, not *four:*

your   pour
you're   yours

Practice speaking, then singing, the following words in sequence:

more ⌢ moor
lore ⌢ lure
pore ⌢ poor

---

[1]For a thorough discussion of *r*, see Lesson 16.

SONG INTERPRETATION AND MUSICIANSHIP
Caccini, "Amarilli, mia bella" ("Amaryllis, My Fair One")

The tempo is marked *Moderato affettuoso*, which means "with moderate movement" *(moderato)* and "tender, passionate expression" *(affettuoso)*. The style of this song is very legato; connect the notes in long lines as in "Caro Mio Ben."

Measures 1–10: Sing as one long phrase within which there are three shorter phrases.

Measures 11–20: Feel these measures as dividing first into four bars, then two, then four more.

Measures 21–27: The composer has written a sequence, a series of repeated ascending figures which lead to a climax.

Note that the song is written in a minor key. Figure out what the key is and what *kind* of minor it is.

On page 216 is another romantic song, this one by the French composer Claude Debussy. Like the Caccini, "Beau soir" should be sung in an intensely legato style and with tenderness. Note how the flowing, harmonically colorful triplets in the accompaniment contribute to the overall effect. Observe in measure 24 the *animando poco a poco e cresc.*, and the *più lento* from measure 33 to the end. The training text contains many diphthongs, including a number of syllables with *fair*, *fear*, and *four* sounds.

Amarilli, mia bella

Amaryllis, My Fair One

Giulio Caccini
1545–1618

Moderato affettuoso

A - ma - ril - li, my fair one, O will you not be-
A - ma - ril - li, mia bel - la, Non cre - di, o del mio

lieve how_____ much I love you, And_____ how much_____
cor dol - ce, de - si - o, d'es - ser tu_____

____ I a - dore you? With all my heart I pledge you
____ l'a - mor mi - o? Cre - di - lo pur; e se ti-

my de - vo - tion; Can you doubt such e - mo - tion?
mar t'as - sa - le, du - bi - tar non ti va - le.

dolce

O - pen your heart,— o hear me I im - plore you! A - ma -
A - pri mi il - pet - to e ve - drai scrit - to in co - re: A - ma -

f
p
smorz.
dolce

cresc.
più cresc.

ril - li, A - ma - ril - li, A - ma -
ril - li, A - ma - ril - li, A - ma -

pp
cresc.
più cresc.

ril - li, I a - dore you! With all my
ril - li, è il mio a - mo - re. Cre - di - lo

heart I pledge you my de - vo - tion,
pur: e se ti - mor t'as - sa - le,

Can you doubt such e-
du - bi - tar non ti

mo - tion? O - pen your heart,___ o hear me I im - plore
va - le, A - pri - mi il pet - to e ve - drai scrit - to in co -

LESSON 13

Consonants Articulated
with the Lips

Webster's New World:	b, p, m, hw, w
American Heritage:	b, p, m, hw, w
International:	b, p, m, hw, w

WORDS WITH THE LIP CONSONANTS

Read aloud slowly:

boat	past	mop	when	wasp
Bob	prop	mob	whip	warm
beam	pent	mime	which	way
bow	prove	mean	what	want

Sing:[1]

1.

boat__ Bob__ beam__ bow__   past__ prop__ pent__ way__   wand
mop__ mob__ mime__ when__   whip__ wasp__ want__ beat__   Bob

2.

boat____ Bob____ beam____ bow____   past____ pop____ prove____ mop
warm____ way____ wand____ beat____   past____ mop____ when____ wasp

---
1. Lesson 13 introduces flexibility studies, vocalises which require the voice to be quite agile. They should be practiced first using vowels and neutral syllables. When they can be sung with reasonable control, the consonant study should be applied.

mop____ mime____ moan____ when____ whip____ which____ what____ wasp
Bob____ prop____ mob____ whip____ warm____ beam____ pent____ mime

3.

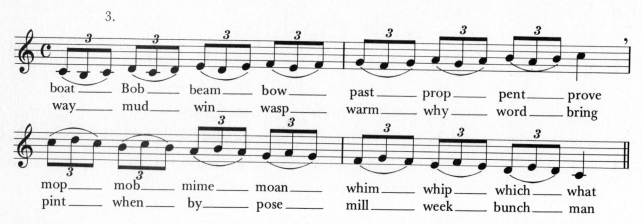

boat____ Bob____ beam____ bow____ past____ prop____ pent____ prove
way____ mud____ win____ wasp____ warm____ why____ word____ bring

mop____ mob____ mime____ moan____ whim____ whip____ which____ what
pint____ when____ by____ pose____ mill____ week____ bunch____ man

4.

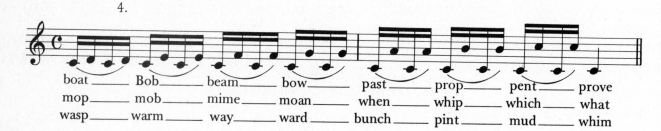

boat____ Bob____ beam____ bow____ past____ prop____ pent____ prove
mop____ mob____ mime____ moan____ when____ whip____ which____ what
wasp____ warm____ way____ ward____ bunch____ pint____ mud____ whim

SENTENCES WITH THE LIP CONSONANTS

Sing until all lip consonants are correctly executed.

1.

ⓐ Bob's____ mom____ went____ past.
ⓑ Which____ one____ went____ west?
ⓒ Pat____ proved____ Mom's____ point.
ⓓ Wasps____ buzz____ when____ mad.

2.

ⓐ Bob's____ mom____ went____ past.
ⓑ Which____ one____ went____ west?
ⓒ Pat____ proved____ Mom's____ point.
ⓓ Wasps____ buzz____ when____ mad.

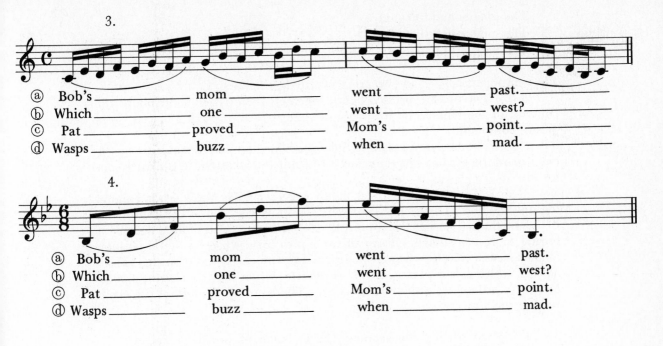

STUDY

The Lip Consonants (b, p, m, hw, w): Description and Execution

Consonants occur before, between, and after vowels. For example, the diphthong $AH\widehat{-IH}$ by itself produces the pronoun *I;* an *n* before and a *t* after the diphthong produces the noun *night (N-AH$\widehat{-IH}$-T);* a *b* before it produces the verb *buy (B-AH$\widehat{-IH}$);* an *s* sound after it produces the noun *ice (AH$\widehat{-IH}$-S).*

There are four general classifications of consonants:

Voiced consonants are those which cause vibration in the vocal bands. To feel these vibrations, place your palm on the top of your head and sing *m, m, m.*

Voiceless consonants are those which do not cause vibration in the vocal bands. Place your palm on your head and sing *p, p, p* with no vowel attached. Note that there is no vibration, only a puff of air.

Stop-plosive consonants are those which have no sustained sound and are followed by a puff of breath. Sing *t, t, t.* Note that this consonant is of short duration and cannot be sustained; it is therefore called *stopped,* which means that a complete closure, or stoppage, of the nasal and oral passages takes place. Because of the sudden release of breath, it is called *plosive,* a word which refers to "the percussive shutting off or release of breath." Stop-plosive consonants may also be voiced. Sing *d, d, d,* or *b, b, b.* Note that these consonants are also stopped and plosive, but that there is a voiced sound.

Continuant consonants have a sustained sound. Sing *m, m, m* again. Note that the nasal passages are open and the sound can be held. The consonant is therefore continuant, not plosive, in character.

Consonants are articulated in six different places. These are:

The lips
The lower lip and upper front teeth
The tip of the tongue

The tongue and the gum
The tongue and the palate
The back of the tongue

The consonants *b, p, m,* and *hw* are articulated as follows:

B (b): The lips are pressed lightly together, then parted suddenly by the emission of the voice. The tip of the tongue is forward; *b* is a voiced, stop-plosive consonant.

P (p): The lips are pressed lightly together, then parted suddenly by the emission of the breath. The tongue is forward; *p* is a voiceless, stop-plosive consonant.

M (m): The lips are pressed lightly together while the voice is emitted through the nose. The tongue is forward; *m* is a voiced, continuant consonant.

HW (hw): The lips are rounded easily forward. After the emission of breath, there is a sudden change of the lips to form whatever vowel position follows: *hw* is a voiceless consonant, articulated with the sound of *h*. Any consonant of which *h* is a part is called an *aspirate*. When used as a verb, *aspirate* means "to pronounce with audible breath." There are two important rules concerning the aspirate:

1.   When singing the aspirate, the emission of breath ceases instantly with the production of the vowel that follows.
2.   The aspirate is always articulated with the mouth shaped for the vowel that follows. For example, sing *he* with the mouth shaped for *EE, hate* with the mouth shaped for *EH,* and *hand* with the mouth shaped for *AH.*

Read the following words aloud; then sing them using the music for the exercises at the beginning of this lesson.

he   hot   whose   hit   hand   heed   hop   hoop   how   have

a) Who has his hoe?
b) Her hair is white.
c) What do they have?

W (w): The lips are rounded easily forward. The tongue is forward. *W* at the beginning of a word is a voiced, continuant consonant. It is identical in execution to the *OO (move)* vowel, but is considered a consonant because the lips widen suddenly to sing the following vowel. At the end of a word, *w* has the character of a vowel *(how, now, cow)*. Sometimes *w* is silent, as in *wring, wrong,* and *wrath.*

The Lip Consonants (b, p, m, hw, w):
Common Faults and Corrections

The most common fault in singing lip consonants is tension in the lips. Relaxed lips result in clearly articulated consonants that can be heard and understood; tense lips cause constriction in the throat, and obscure and muddle the diction. When the lips are completely relaxed the throat tends to be relaxed, with the result that the tone is clear, the diction understandable. Practice speaking and singing the lip consonants with lips so relaxed that they feel flabby and rubber-like. Master this principle before proceeding to the next lesson.

To sing the consonants:

B: Do not protrude the lips or press them tightly together. Do not substitute *m* for *b* (sounding as though you have a cold). Note that in words ending in *mb*, *b* is silent (*climb, thumb, limb*). Do not sing a nonexistent *m* when *b* begins a word (*m-because, m-beautiful*). Sing *b* clearly in *pp* passages. When *b* occurs before a consonant sound or a stop (rest, breathing place, dramatic pause), it is followed by the vowel sound *UH*. When *UH* is inaudible, *b* is also inaudible. For example:

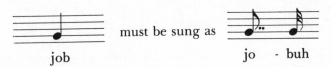

Caution: Sing *UH* on exactly the same pitch as *b*.

P: Relax the lips; do not press them tightly together. Note that *p* and *b* are similarly executed. Do not sing, "My bent-up (pent-up) emotions" or "Let us bray (pray)." Remember that *p* is not voiced.

P is difficult to articulate when it precedes *t*, as in *capture, rapture,* and *scripture.* Practice singing these words by over-aspirating the *p* consonant. Similarly, over-aspirate *p* before any consonant sound.

M: Do not tighten the lips; they should be relaxed and barely touching. *M* (like *n*) is a humming consonant which, when properly executed, can lend smoothness, expressiveness, and resonance to your singing. It can help make phrases coherent by connecting vowels and words. For example, "O moon" and "Come to me" can often be sung as follows:

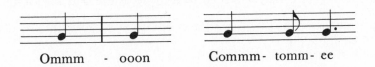

Note that *m* takes part of the time from the preceding vowel.

Caution: When *m* occurs between two vowels of different pitch,

it is sung on the pitch of the first vowel *only*, regardless of which is the higher or lower. *Do not sing* m *on the second pitch or on both pitches.*

When *m* follows a consonant sound (*that mob, his mother*), do not attempt to prolong it. When *m* precedes a consonant sound or a stop, it should be prolonged, but another vowel should not be inserted ("The thirst that from-uh the soul doth rise"; "Going home - uh, going home - uh"); keep the lips closed until the next consonant is sounded. __

Hw and *w:* Do not let the $\overline{OO}$ vowel become a part of *hw*. For this consonant sound, the lips are shaped for $\overline{OO}$, but breath, not tone, is sent through the lips. When *w* begins a word, there is a momentary $\overline{OO}$ sound, but the lips must move quickly to the vowel that follows. Do not confuse *hw* and *w* by singing *witch* for *which*, and *wear* for *where*. Remember that *hw* is aspirated, *w* is voiced.

SONG INTERPRETATION AND MUSICIANSHIP
Bach, "If Thou Be Near" ("Bist du bei mir")

This selection calls for a legato style. Practice legato by singing each phrase on a single vowel; then repeat the phrase with words, retaining the "connected" feeling. Thus, measures 5–8 would first be practiced:

Mah _____   Mah _____

The consonants *m* and *n* help to produce sustained sound. Where these consonants occur, use them to secure a better legato.

"If Thou Be Near" is a Baroque composition. Review upbeat phrasing in Lesson 8; bring that principle to this song.

On page 220 is a fine song for male voice by the English composer Ralph Vaughan Williams. "The Vagabond" is the first of nine songs on texts by R. L. Stevenson which the composer published under the title *Songs of Travel*. The entire cycle is worthy of study and fun to sing.

Bach is considered by many to be the greatest composer of all time. His musical output was astounding, in terms of both quantity and quality, yet "If Thou Be Near," which was dedicated to his wife, is the only love song that he wrote.

If Thou Be Near

Bist du bei mir

Johann Sebastian Bach
(1685–1750)

1.Training text: If thou be near, then I wait calm - ly

2.German text: Bist du bei mir, geh' ich mit Freu - den

to greet___ my___ death with grate - ful___ heart, to___

zum Ster - ben___ und zu mei - ner___ Ruh', zum___

greet my death with grate - ful heart.
Ster - ben und zu mei - ner Ruh'!

If thou__ be__
Bist du__ bei__

near,
mir,

then I wait calm - ly to greet__ my
geh' ich mit Freu - den zum Ster - ben__

death with grate - ful__ heart, to__ greet my death with grate - ful
und zu mei - ner__ Ruh', zum__ Ster - ben und zu mei - ner

O hap - py life, O per - fect end - ing,
Ach, wie ver-gnügt wär' so mein En - de,

with thy___ blest___ hand u - pon___ my___ brow___ when at___
es drück - ten___ dei - ne lie - ben___ Hän - de mir___

last my eye - lids close in death. If thou___ be___ near,
die ge - treu - en Au - gen zu! Bist du___ bei___ mir,

then I wait calm - ly, to greet my death with grate-ful
geh' ich mit Freu - den, *zum Ster - ben und zu mei - ner*

heart, to greet my death with grate - ful heart.
Ruh', *zum Ster - ben und zu mei - ner Ruh'!*

LESSON 14

Consonants Articulated
with the Lower Lip
and Upper Teeth

Webster's New World:	f, v
American Heritage:	f, v
International:	f, v

WORDS WITH THE LIP-TEETH CONSONANTS

Read aloud slowly:

fit	food	vow	grieve	fill	soft	view	brave
fall	oft	vast	voice	fair	laugh	verse	of

Sing:

1.

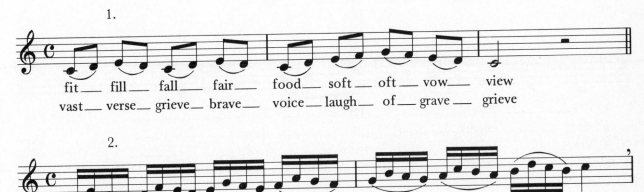

fit ___ fill ___ fall ___ fair ___ food ___ soft ___ oft ___ vow ___ view
vast ___ verse ___ grieve ___ brave ___ voice ___ laugh ___ of ___ grave ___ grieve

2.

fit _____ fall _____ food _____ oft _____ vow _____ vast _____ grieve _____ voice

fill _____ fair _____ soft _____ laugh _____ view _____ verse _____ brave _____ of

3.

fit_____ fill_____ fall_____ fair_____   food_____ soft_____ off_____ laugh

vow_____ view_____ vast_____ verse_____   grieve_____ brave_____ voice_____ of

4.

fit_____ fill_____ fall_____ fair_____   food_____ soft_____ off_____ laugh
vow_____ view_____ vast_____ verse_____   grieve_____ have_____ voice_____ of

SENTENCES WITH THE LIP-TEETH CONSONANTS

Sing until all consonants are clearly executed.

1.

ⓐ Ralph_____ fought_____ Jeff_____ Ford.
ⓑ Soft _____ laughs_____ foil _____ fear.
ⓒ Vines_____ freeze _____ from _____ frost.
ⓓ Love_____ vows_____ oft'_____ fail.

2.

ⓐ Ralph_____ fought _____   Jeff_____ Ford._____
ⓑ Soft_____ laughs _____   foil _____ fear._____
ⓒ Vines_____ freeze _____   from _____ frost._____
ⓓ Love _____ vows_____   oft'_____ fail._____

3.

ⓐ Ralph_____ fought_____ Jeff _____ Ford._____ ⓑ Soft _____ laughs_____ foil _____ fear._____
ⓒ Vines _____ freeze _____ from_____ frost._____ ⓓ Love _____ vows _____ oft'_____ fail._____

4.

ⓐ Ralph_____   fought_____   Jeff_____   Ford.
ⓑ Soft_____   laughs_____   foil_____   fear.
ⓒ Vines_____   freeze_____   from_____   frost.
ⓓ Love_____   vows_____   oft'_____   fail.

STUDY

The Lip-Teeth Consonants (f, v): Description and Execution

F (f), a voiceless continuant, is articulated as follows:

1.   The inside of the lower lip touches the upper front teeth.
2.   While this position is held, the breath is emitted through the mouth.
3.   The tip of the tongue is forward.

Articulate *V* (v), a voiced continuant, as follows:

1.   The lower lip touches the upper front teeth.
2.   While this position is held, the voice is emitted through the mouth.
3.   The tongue is forward.

F and *V* are articulated in the same place and in the same manner; they differ in that *f* is voiceless and *v* is voiced. Many consonants are similar to others. Learn to recognize the distinctive characteristics of each. Ask the following questions about each consonant:

1.   *Where* is it articulated?
2.   *How* is it articulated?
3.   Is it *voiced* or *voiceless?*

The Lip-Teeth Consonants (f, v): Common Faults and Corrections

F: Keep the lips relaxed. Do not bite into the lower lip or tighten it. Raise the upper lip. Avoid any vocalized sound.

When *f* is followed by a syllable or word beginning with a vowel sound, it must be sounded at the beginning of that syllable or word. For example, sing *o-ften,*[1] not *of-ten,* and *a-ffair,* not *aff-air.*

When *f* is followed by a consonant, the vowel preceding *f* should be sustained for its full duration, and *f* should be executed just before the consonant. For example, sing *if thou* as *i-fthou,* and *safe passage* as *sa-fepassage.*

When *f* occurs at the end of a word, do not add a vowel *(safe-uh, grief-uh).* Avoid this by keeping the lower lip and upper teeth together until the breath for *f* has stopped.

---

1.   The *t* in *often* is silent.

V: The common faults in singing *f* also apply to *v.* The point of contact between the lower lip and upper teeth for singing *v* differs with people because facial structure, size, and shape of lips and teeth differ. Find the point of contact that produces a relaxed, resonant *v.* Do not tense the lips.

When *v* occurs between two vowel sounds on the same pitch, it should be connected to the first. Sing *viv-id,* not *vi-vid,* and *ev-il,* not *e-vil.* When *v* occurs between two vowel sounds of different pitches, it is always sung on the lower pitch:

Caution: Do not "slide" or "scoop." Sing *v* only on the lower pitch.

When *v* occurs at the end of a word before either a stop or another word beginning with a consonant, do not allow an *uh* to sound (I *love-uh* you, *leave-uh* me). Stop the voice before the lower lip and upper teeth separate.

SONG INTERPRETATION AND MUSICIANSHIP

Caldara, "Come raggio di sol" ("As from the Shining Sun")

This song must be sung in an extremely sustained, legato style. Although you were cautioned not to scoop or slide, true Italian style not only permits this type of connection but demands it. Imagine the sound that is produced when a fine violinist slides his finger on the fingerboard in order to connect two tones. The voice should slide from one tone to another in much the same manner here. If you listen to recordings of fine singers singing Italian art songs or opera, the style will immediately become apparent. To help in your initial attempts, dotted slurs have been drawn between notes in the song; where these appear, the voice should glide from one pitch to the next.

Timing in attack and duration of syllables and words are important considerations for singing "in tempo," and this requires two basic techniques:

1. Vowels must begin precisely when their notes begin.
2. Consonants and unstressed diphthong sounds must be articulated before or after the vowels.

The following examples will help to make these techniques clear.

Example 1 shows the melody of measures 4–7 of "Come raggio di sol." Note that only the vowels from the training text have been included; consonants and unstressed diphthong sounds have been omitted. Sing this example with vowels only, making certain each is attacked precisely when the note above it should begin.

In example 2, the consonants and unstressed diphthong sounds have been added so that they occur before, after, and between the notes. Sing this example, making certain that the vowels are articulated at exactly the same time as they were in example 1. All syllables and words should now flow in tempo.

Instrumentalists do not have these problems, since they activate a reed, string, or column of air and produce sound almost instantly. But when singing English, a language containing eleven vowels, nine diphthongs, and six kinds of consonants in many combinations, one must master the attack and proper duration of many sounds. Otherwise notes will appear late, which will be particularly evident when singing with instrumental accompaniment or in a chorus. Even professional soloists must sometimes be reminded of this fact.

Review all the songs you have learned, making certain that you "vowel in tempo."

Memorize the following:

tranquillo: in a tranquil, restful manner
stent. (stentato): hard, forced, loud, labored
dim. assai (diminuendo assai): much softer
simile: in like manner
ppp (pianississimo): as soft as possible
col canto: with the melody

Measures 4–5: Do not sing in a static, "beaty" fashion. A group of repeated notes usually leads to a climax note and is sung with a slight crescendo. Sing "through" these measures, as well as measures 8–9, 12–13, 16–17, 22–23, 25–26, 36–37, and 39–40.

Measure 16: In addition to accelerating the speed slightly, intensify the vocal sound and color the voice with a feeling of agitation. Do not employ much volume before measures 23–27.

Measure 28: Establish a new mood here, in contrast to the earlier mood of serenity and calm.

Measure 36: Observe the stress markings (–), singing with a slightly weighted, heavier tone.

Note to the accompanist: The piano accompaniment is to be played *semi-legato* ( ) throughout.

Along with "Come raggio di sol," study César Franck's famous sacred song "O Lord Most Holy" (p. 226). This song requires a broad, spun-out vocal line. Sing with reverence and emotion. Make the vocal line "fit" the tempo of the underlying eighth notes in the accompaniment.

Caldara was a contemporary of the two great Baroque masters Handel and Bach, and his music reflects the same traditions. Although he worked in Vienna, he was Italian both in origin and schooling. He composed 87 operas, 36 oratorios, and much fine church and instrumental music. He had a deep love of euphony and expressiveness, which resulted in a lovely, flowing, melodic style. "Come raggio di sol" is perhaps his most famous song.

Come raggio di sol
As from the Shining Sun

Antonio Caldara
(1670–1736)

Sostenuto

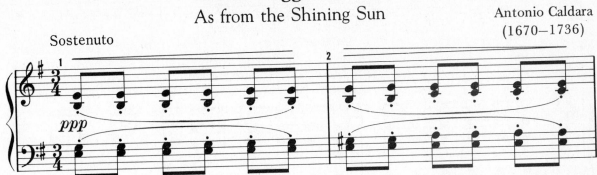

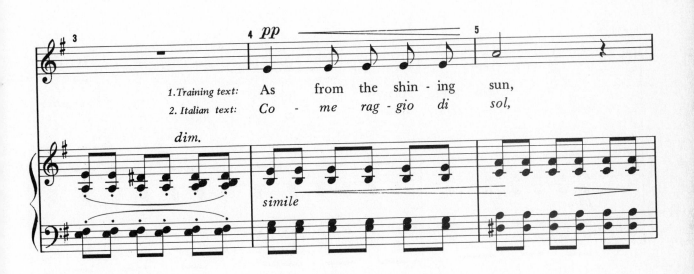

1. Training text: As from the shin - ing sun,
2. Italian text: Co - me rag - gio di sol,

soft - ly re - flec - ted,   as from the shin - ing
mi - te e se - re - no,   co - me rag - gio di

135

sun,   soft - ly re - flec - ted,

sol,   mi - te e se - re - no,

sun - beams play - ful - ly flut - ter on the

so - vra pla - ci - di flut - ti si ri -

rip - plets,   while in the o - cean, while

po - sa,   men - tre del ma - re, men -

affrett. poco a poco

136

LESSON 15

Consonants Articulated with the Tip of the Tongue

Webster's New World:	th, t, d, n, l
American Heritage:	th, t, d, n, l
International:	(θ, ð) t, d, n, l

WORDS WITH THE TIP-OF-TONGUE CONSONANTS

Read aloud slowly:

throw	taught	do	new	leap
thing	two	die	none	late
them	shut	done	not	shall
the	fit	and	need	will

Sing:

1.

thing__ throw__ them __ the ____ two __ fit __ taught __ die ____ do
and __ done__ none __ new__ need __ late__ leap __ will ____ shall
shut __ not ___ thing __ fit ____ thing __ throw__ none __ will ____ die

2.

throw____ taught __ do ____ new ____ leap____ thing _____ two____ die

none ____ late ____ them ____ shut ____ done ____ not ____ shall ____ and

3.

thing ____ throw ____ them ____ two ____ fit ____ taught ____ die ____ do

none ____ new ____ need ____ not ____ late ____ leap ____ will ____ shall

4.

thing ____ throw ____ two ____ fit ____ die ____ do ____ none ____ new
late ____ leap ____ them ____ the ____ taught ____ and ____ need ____ will

SENTENCES WITH THE TIP-OF-TONGUE CONSONANTS

Sing until all consonants are clearly executed.

1.

(a) Think _____ through _____ these _____ truths.
(b) Tom _____ bought _____ two _____ tunes.
(c) Dan _____ danced _____ 'til _____ dawn.
(d) Ned _____ said _____ "Kneel _____ now."
(e) Nell _____ will _____ leave _____ late.

2.

(a) Think _____ through _____ these _____ truths. _____
(b) Tom _____ bought _____ two _____ tunes. _____
(c) Dan _____ danced _____ 'til _____ dawn. _____
(d) Ned _____ said _____ "Kneel _____ now." _____
(e) Nell _____ will _____ leave _____ late. _____

3.

(a) Think _____ through _____ these _____ truths. _ (b) Tom _____ bought _____ two _____ tunes. _____
(c) Dan _____ danced _____ 'til _____ dawn. _ (d) Ned _____ said _____ "Kneel _____ now." _____
(e) Nell _____ will _____ leave _____ late. _ (f) Will _____ they _____ quiet _____ down? _____

4.

(a) Think	_____	through	_____	these	_____	truths.
(b) Tom	_____	bought	_____	two	_____	tunes.
(c) Dan	_____	danced	_____	'til	_____	dawn.
(d) Ned	_____	said	_____	"Kneel	_____	now."
(e) Nell	_____	will	_____	leave	_____	late.

STUDY
The Tip-of-Tongue Consonants (th, t, d, n, l): Description and Execution

Th (th) is a continuant and may be voiced or voiceless. It is sung as follows:

1. The tip of the tongue is placed lightly against the edge of the upper front teeth.
2. When *th* is voiced, the *voice* is emitted over the tongue.
3. When *th* is voiceless, the *breath* is emitted over the tongue.

Th is voiced in the following:

this   rather   that   brother   the   bother   with[1]   mother

Th is voiceless in the following:

thing   thank   throw   thin   tenth   twelfth   author   Keith

When *th* is voiceless, it is an aspirate.

T (t) is voiceless and stop-plosive. Articulate *t* as follows:

1. Place the tip of the tongue lightly against the gums of the upper front teeth.
2. Drop the tongue quickly, and at the same time emit a puff of breath over it.

D (d) is voiced and stop-plosive. Sing *d* as follows:

1. The tip of the tongue is flattened against the gums of the upper front teeth.

---

1. Optionally voiced in speech, but always in singing.

2. Drop the tongue quickly, and at the same time emit the voice over it.

N (n) is a voiced, nasal continuant, and is sung as follows:

1. The tip of the tongue is flattened against the gums of the upper front teeth.
2. While this position is held, the voice is emitted through the nose.

L (l) is a voiced continuant. Sing *l* as follows:

1. The tip of the tongue is placed lightly against the gum of the upper front teeth.
2. The front of the tongue is spread widely against the hard palate.
3. While this position is held, the voice is emitted over the sides of the tongue.

The Tip-of-Tongue Consonants (θ, ð, t, d, n, l): Common Faults and Corrections

Th: Use only the tip of the tongue, avoiding tightness and rigidity at the base. Move the tongue quickly, or a thick, guttural sound will result.

In voiceless *th,* exaggerate the aspiration slightly or the word will not be understood. Without the sound of breath, one would sing *burr* for *birth,* and *wrong* for *throng.*

In voiced *th,* exaggerate the vocalized sound; without this sound, one sings *eye* for *thy,* and *us* for *thus.*

An extraneous vowel should not sound when *th* follows *n* or *l (on - uh these, all - uh things).* To avoid this, use the same tongue position for *n* and *l* as for *th.* For example, when singing *on these,* allow the tip of the tongue to extend outside the edge of the upper front teeth. *N, l,* and *th* can be articulated from this position; the tongue does not have to be moved twice.

Caution: For *l,* even though the same position is used, the tongue tip must move back at the instant *th* is sounded.

The tongue position described above should be used when *ths* appears at the end of the word so that *th* is not omitted. Sing *truths,* not *trues,* and *mouths,* not *mouze.*

When *th* occurs before a syllable or a vowel sound, it should be connected with that syllable or vowel sound. Sing *mo - ther,* not *moth - er,* and *no - thing,* not *noth - ing.*

When voiceless *th* is followed by a consonant or a stop, do not add an extraneous vowel sound *(death - uh with, my last breath - uh).* Exaggerate the puff of breath, keeping the tongue in position until the breath is stopped. Observe the same rule for voiced *th* before a consonant or a stop.

T: This consonant is often omitted or sung inaudibly. To articulate *t,* the tongue tip should be activated where the upper gum ridge curves into the hard palate. Do not flatten the tongue or allow it to touch the teeth. Make the puff of breath accompanying *t* audible; otherwise *d* will be sounded. Do not sing *bedder* for *better,* or *sidder* for *sitter.* The tongue moves quickly, darting away from the upper gum ridge at the moment of aspiration. *Do not omit* t *at the ends of words.* Sing *guest* rather than *guess, wait* rather than *weigh,* and *blessed*[2] rather than *bless.* Exaggerate *t* when practicing these words.

---

2. Note that *-ed* is pronounced *t* when it occurs after a voiceless consonant in one-syllable words.

When *t* occurs before a vowel or syllable, it is attached to that vowel or syllable. For example, sing *be - tter,* not *bett - er,* and *i-tis,* not *it is.* Exaggerate the puff of breath accompanying *t* before a consonant or a stop *(waiT for me, she is sweeT),* but do not allow another vowel to sound *(wait - uh for me, she is sweet - uh).* Articulate *t* a split second before the consonant. Do not allow vocalized sound to accompany *t* before the stop.

When *t* occurs at the beginning of a final syllable, it must be clearly articulated. Sing *li-ttle,* not *lill,* and *bea-ten,* not *bean.*

D: D is a voiced consonant. With two exceptions discussed below, *d* and *t* are similarly articulated. Do not confuse the two: *d* requires voice, *t* requires breath.

D is treated exactly like *b* (Lesson 13) before a stop or consonant—that is, the vowel *uh* must accompany *d.* Without *uh,* there is no *d.*

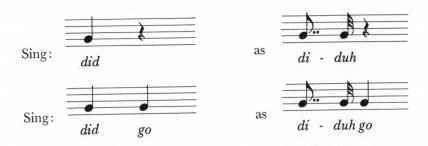

Sing: *did* as *di - duh*

Sing: *did go* as *di - duh go*

Many words in English end with *d.* Unless the technique described above is mastered, these words will not be understood.

Caution: When *d* ends a word preceding another word beginning with *d,* the *uh* sound is unnecessary since only one *d* is sounded. Sing *and die* as *an - die,* not *and - uh die.*

N: The rules for singing *n* are much the same as those for singing *m* (Lesson 13). Prolong *n* whenever possible. Sing *n* between vowels on the pitch of the first vowel only to avoid scooping. Avoid an *uh* sound when *n* precedes a consonant *(Drink to me on - uh - ly).* When *n* occurs at the end of a word, keep the tongue in position until the tone is stopped.

L: When *l* occurs before or between vowel sounds, it is connected to the vowel sound that it precedes. Sing *lu - lla - by,* not *lull - a - by,* and *me - lo - dy,* not *mel - o - dy.* Do not prolong *l* when it precedes a vowel or appears between vowels. This causes a throaty tone and tends to muddle the diction. Articulate *l* quickly by a flip of the tongue.

When *l* occurs after a vowel, it *should* be prolonged, and the tongue *should not* be flipped. Without a prolonged *l,* the sense of many words will be lost. If the tongue is flipped, an unnecessary *uh* will be heard. Sing *yell,* not *yea* or *yell - uh; isle,* not *I* or *isle - uh;* and *wills,* not *wiz* or *wills - uh.* Keep the tongue in position for *l* until the tone is stopped.

Take care to execute *l* clearly when it precedes *d.* Do not sing *mode* for *mold,* and *rode* for *rolled.*

L is sometimes silent. Do not sing the *l* in words such as *talk, walk, psalm, folk,* and *half.*

Do not diphthongize pure vowels that precede *l.* Avoid singing *dee - uhl* for *deal* and *roo - uhl* for *rule.* Move the tongue into position for *l* at the instant that *l* is sounded.

SONG INTERPRETATION AND MUSICIANSHIP
R. Strauss, "The Night" ("Die Nacht")

This is a dramatic mood piece calling for a sensitive relationship between the melody and the accompaniment.

Memorize the following:

Sotto voce: softly; in an undertone
Una corda: use the soft pedal on the piano

Measures 2–17: Sing without using the full voice. Use a *mezzo voce* production. Allow the vocal line to blend with the accompaniment.

Measures 15 and 24: Sing delicately. A light, almost breathy quality will provide the best coloring.

Measures 18–24: Add more movement and a brighter tone. Distinguish between ♪ ♪ and ♪. ♪ .

Measures 28–30: Add more weight to the tone. The feeling, however, should be of breadth rather than loudness.

Measures 34–40: Note that the climax is reached at *pp*.

Measures 41–45: This is the postlude. Do not break the mood until the piano concludes.

A complete contrast to the dramatic intensity of "The Night" is DePue's "Lullaby" on page 231. Sing this song very simply and quite softly. For another lullaby, sing the famous one by Brahms on page 234.

Richard Strauss was one of the greatest figures in music around the turn of the century. He was a prominent composer, a master orchestrator, and an expert conductor. He developed the symphonic poem to its highest form, and wrote highly successful operas and many beautiful songs. "The Night" is from his Opus 10, *Acht Gedichte (Eight Poems)*, one of his earlier compositions.

The Night
Die Nacht

Hermann von Gilm

Richard Strauss
(1864 - 1949)

1. Training text: Comes the night _____ o'er hill and dell,
2. German text: Aus dem Wal - de tritt die Nacht,

Dark-'ning woods that once were light - ed;
aus dem Bäu - men schleicht sie lei - se,

Now, be-hold, the
schaut sich um in

day has end - ed, dark - ness reigns!
wei - tem Krei - se, nun gib Acht.

we would hold, cov - ers sil - ver from the stream,
was nur hold, nimmt das Sil - ber weg des Stroms,

cov - ers can - dle's light a - gleam, all the gold!
nimmt von Kup - fer - dach des Doms weg das Gold.

Ped. ✳

p   dim.

Ped.   ✳ Ped.   ✳

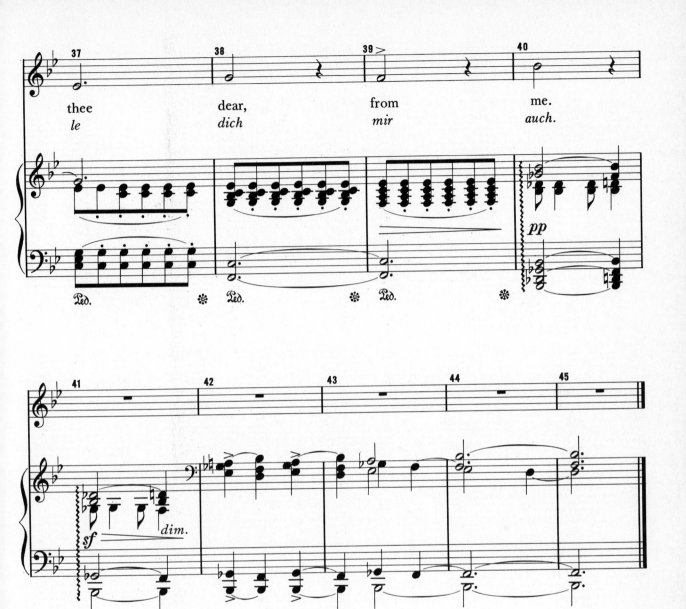

thee   dear,   from   me.
le   *dich*   *mir*   *auch.*

Consonants Articulated with the Tongue and Gum

Webster's New World:	s, z, sh, zh, r
American Heritage:	s, z, sh, zh, r
International:	s, z, ʃ, ʒ, r

WORDS WITH THE TONGUE AND GUM CONSONANTS

Read aloud slowly:

sing	zest	show	azure	run
pass	zeal	push	vision	breath
see	poise	hush	pleasure	cry
so	choose	short	leisure	far

Sing:

sing— zest — vi - sion a - zure run — pass — zeal — push — see
poise— hush— plea - sure lei - sure show— far — cry— short — so

sing —— pass —— see —— so —— zest —— zeal —— choose —— vi - sion

run ____ breath ____ cry ____ push ____ show ____ hush ____ poise ____ lei - sure

3.

sing ____ pass ____ see ____ zest ____ zeal ____ poise ____ show ____ push

hush ____ a - zure ____ vi - sion ____ run ____ cry ____ far

4.

so ____ choose ____ short ____ lei - sure ____ far ____ sing ____ zest - a - zure
show ____ run ____ pass ____ vi - sion ____ zeal ____ push ____ breath plea - sure

SENTENCES WITH THE TONGUE AND GUM CONSONANTS

Sing until all consonants are clearly executed.

1.

(a) She ____ sings ____ sweet ____ songs. ____
(b) Please ____ choose ____ his ____ clothes. ____
(c) Lei - sure ____ some - times ____ mea - sures ____ plea - sure. ____
(d) Shops ____ sell ____ sea ____ shells. ____
(e) Girls ____ user ____ red ____ rouge. ____

2.

(a) She ____ sings ____ sweet ____ songs. ____
(b) Please ____ choose ____ his ____ clothes. ____
(c) Shops ____ sell ____ sea ____ shells. ____
(d) Lei - sure ____ some - times ____ mea - sures ____ plea - sure. ____
(e) Girls ____ use ____ red ____ rouge. ____

3.

(a) She___ sings___ sweet___ songs.__ (b) Please____ choose____ his ____ clothes. ___

(c) Shops___ sell ___ sea ___ shells.__ (d) Lei - sure_ some-times_ mea - sures_ plea - sure.

(e) Girls___ use ___ red ___ rouge. (f) She ____ has ____ a - zure eyes.____

4.

(a) She____ sings ____ sweet ____ songs.____

(b) Please ____ choose ____ his ____ clothes. ____

(c) Shops ____ sell ____ sea ____ shells.____

(d) Lei - sure some - times mea - sures plea - sure.

(e) Girls ____ use ____ red ____ rouge. ____

STUDY

The Tongue and Gum Consonants (s, z, sh, zh, r): Description and Execution

The consonant *s*(s), sometimes spelled *c*, is a voiceless continuant. Sing *s* as follows:

1. The tip of the tongue is raised toward, but does not touch, the center of the upper front teeth.
2. The sides of the tongue are against the upper side teeth.
3. While this position is held, the breath is emitted over the groove of the tongue and between the nearly closed front teeth.

S is a sibilant.
Z(z), sometimes spelled *s*, is a voiced continuant, and is sung as follows:

1. The tip of the tongue is raised toward, but does not touch, the center of the upper front teeth.
2. The sides of the tongue are against the upper side teeth.
3. While this position is held, the voice is emitted over the groove of the tongue and between the nearly closed front teeth.

S and *z* differ only in that *s* is voiceless and *z* is voiced.
Sh(sh) is a voiceless continuant and is articulated as follows:

1. The tip of the tongue is raised slightly higher than for *s*, toward the center of the upper front teeth.
2. The sides of the tongue are placed against the edges of the upper side teeth.
3. While this position is held, the breath is emitted forcefully over the tongue and between nearly closed front teeth.

Sh is a sibilant.

Zh(zh) is a voiced continuant and is sung as follows:

1. The tip of the tongue is raised slightly higher than for *s*, toward the center of the upper front teeth.
2. The sides of the tongue are placed against the edges of the upper side teeth.
3. While this position is held, the voice is emitted over the tongue and between nearly closed front teeth.

Sh and *zh* differ only in that *sh* is voiceless and *zh* is voiced.

R(r) may be a voiced continuant, or it may be tongued. As a voiced continuant, *r* is sung as follows:

1. The tip of the tongue is pointed toward the back of the upper front gums.
2. The back of the tongue is down.
3. While this position is held, the voice is emitted over the tongue.

Execute tongued *r* as follows:

1. The tip of the tongue darts against the upper front gums, touching only once.
2. The back of the tongue is down.

In the United States, *r* is generally sung as a voiced continuant; tongued *r* is commonly used in England.

The Tongue and Gum Consonants (s, z, ʃ, ʒ, r): Common Faults and Corrections

S and *z:* These consonants do not usually present problems except to those who lisp. Lisping is usually caused by incorrect tongue or lip position. The tip of the tongue must be in the center of the mouth, close to the upper teeth, but not touching. Do not place the tongue tip against the lower gum or teeth. Hold the sides of the tongue against the upper side teeth, or breath will escape laterally. Do not attempt to emit the breath too forcefully. Keep the lips in an oval, relaxed position. Check with a hand mirror to avoid a crooked lip position.

When *s* or *z* is followed by a syllable or a word beginning with a vowel, it is attached to that syllable or vowel. Sing *pa - ssing*, not *pass - ing*, and *ri - zup*, not *rise up*.

When *s* or *z* is followed by a consonant or a stop, do not add *uh*. Sing *ki - ssme*, not *kiss - uh me*, *choo - zyour*, not *choose - uh your*, and *arose*, not *arose - uh*. Do not move the tongue until the breath or tone stops.

When *s* ends a word before a word beginning with *s*, only one prolonged *s* is sounded. *Let us see* is sung, *Le - tu - see*. The same rule applies to *z*.

When *s . . . z* or *z . . . s* occurs together, do not try to separate them. Merge the two sounds *(Hiszeal)*.

Sh(ʃ) and *zh*(ʒ): Make certain that *sh* is aspirated and *zh* is voiced. When either is followed by a syllable or by a word beginning with a vowel, it is attached to that syllable or vowel. Sing *pu - shing*, not *push - ing*, and *vi - sion*, not *vis - ion*.

Do not allow an *uh* to sound when *sh* or *zh* precedes a consonant or a stop. Sing *hu - shnow*, not *hush - uh now*, and *prestige*, not *prestige - uh*.

When *sh* precedes another *sh* ("And all flesh shall see it together"), merge the two into a single prolonged *sh*.

R: Omit r *before a consonant sound or stop.* If a clear voiced *r* is sung, the vowel preceding *r* will be distorted by the movement of the tongue upwards.

If tongued *r* is sung, diction sounds affected and artificial.

In the following words, notice that when *r* is omitted before a consonant or stop, a diphthong is sounded:

lord	is sung	*law ⌐ uh(r)d*
arm	is sung	*ah ⌐ uh(r)m*
morning	is sung	*maw ⌐ uh(r)ning*
for you	is sung	*faw ⌐ uh(r) you*
near me	is sung	*nih ⌐ uh(r) me*
their love	is sung	*theh ⌐ uh(r) love*

To achieve clarity on extremely high tones, even before a consonant or stop, sing tongued *r*.

The vowel preceding an omitted *r* is prolonged for its full value and is pure. *Park* is sung *pah - uh(r)k*, not *pock*; *mark* is *mah - uh(r)k*, not *mock*. When *r* ends a word before another word beginning with *r*, the first *r* is omitted and the second sounded as a voiced continuant.

Always sing r *before a vowel sound* and attach it to that vowel sound:

a - round	not	*ar - ound*
bo - rrow	not	*bor - row*
spi - rit	not	*spir - it*
fo - rall	not	*for all*

Sing tongued *r* in opera and between vowel sounds in sacred and art songs. In all other music, sing voiced *r*.

Never use tongued *r* in popular songs, American folk songs, musical comedy (excepting Gilbert and Sullivan), or patriotic songs, since it will sound affected and pretentious.

When *r* follows *t* or *d (train, trip, drain, drip)*, it is voiced, even in opera, art, or sacred song.

When *cr* or *gr* combinations occur in dramatic or colorful words *(cry, cruel, grief, great)*, use tongued *r*.

Avoid "burring" in voiced *r*. Keep the back of the tongue down, away from the palate, to avoid a guttural, flat, burred sound.

SONG INTERPRETATION AND MUSICIANSHIP
D'Hardelot, "Because"

A favorite since it was composed, "Because" continues to be a popular solo for weddings. Its romantic, sentimental quality permits more freedom of interpretation than is usual in songs of the classical or even the romantic period. Some liberties of tempo and dynamics are allowable, but they should not be excessive.

Measure 9: Clap the rhythm ♩.♪♪.♪♪♪♪ and speak the words in this rhythm before singing. This pattern occurs several times (measures 15, 17, 19, 30). After the basic rhythm is mastered in strict tempo, sing, using the rubato style. Each time the measure is repeated, stress a different word or note. Keep the underlying beat steady.

Measure 15: Do not "bounce" the sixteenth notes; keep them as connected as possible.

Measures 17–19: These phrases are rhythmically similar to measure 15. Each succeeding group is to be performed more loudly and intensely.

Measure 19: Sing with rubato.

Measures 21–24: If the long high note cannot be sustained, breathe after the word *because* in measure 21.

Measure 25: Sing broadly, with full resonance.

Two more songs at the back of the book are recommended for study. The first (p. 236) is "Silent Noon" by Ralph Vaughan Williams. This song contrasts sharply in style with "The Vagabond." It requires excellent control of breath and tone, since its phrases are long, with many dynamic changes. Sing this song first on a neutral syllable, then with text, being careful not to force the voice. Seek to exercise complete control of the breath, with firm support for every tone.

The second song, on page 241, is the well-known aria "O Rest in the Lord," from the oratorio *Elijah* by Mendelssohn. Sing quietly, with warm simplicity. This is a three-part song. The middle section, beginning in measure 12, may be sung a bit faster than the beginning, but return to the original tempo in measure 20. Observe the *Lento* in measure 32.

Because

English words by
Edward Teschemacher

Guy d'Hardelot
(1858–1936)

Be - cause _____ God made thee
Et puis _____ tu viens à

mine, _____ I'll cher - ish thee _____ Through
moi _____ et je fris - son - ne, Tu

light and dark - ness, through all time to be, _____ And
prends ma main, et tout mon coeur se don - ne A

Consonants Articulated with the Tongue and Hard Palate

Webster's New World:	y, ch, j
American Heritage:	y, ch, j
International:	j, tʃ, dʒ

WORDS WITH THE TONGUE AND HARD-PALATE CONSONANTS

Read aloud slowly:

yes	charm	June
yet	chance	just
yield	such	age
yearn	choose	ridge

Sing:

1.

yes — charm — June — yet — chance — just — yield — such — age.
yearn — choose — ridge — such — charm — June — age — yet — yes.

2.

choose — such — chance — charm — ridge — age — just — June

yearn ____ yield ____ yet ____ yes ____ chance ____ age ____ such ____ yet.

3.

yes ____ yet ____ yield ____ yearn ____ charm ____ chance ____ such ____ choose

June ____ just ____ age ____ ridge ____ yawn ____ yore ____ cheer ____ jaw

4.

yes ____ yet ____ yield ____ yearn ____ charm ____ chance ____ such ____ choose

June ____ just ____ age ____ ridge ____ youth ____ chaste ____ jaw ____ chin

SENTENCES WITH THE TONGUE AND HARD-PALATE CONSONANTS

Sing until all consonants are clearly executed:

1.

(a) You ____ use ____ your ____ yacht.
(b) Chimes ____ charm ____ church - es.
(c) John's ____ grudge ____ jolts ____ Jill.
(d) Age ____ chides ____ youth's ____ cheer.

2.

(a) You ____ use ____ your ____ yacht. ____
(b) Chimes ____ charm ____ church - es. ____
(c) John's ____ grudge ____ jolts ____ Jill. ____
(d) Age ____ chides ____ youth's ____ cheer. ____

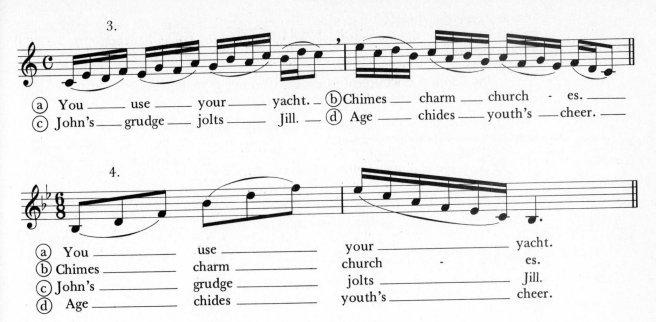

a) You ____ use ____ your ____ yacht. _ b) Chimes ____ charm ____ church - es. ____
c) John's ____ grudge ____ jolts ____ Jill. _ d) Age ____ chides ____ youth's ____ cheer. ____

a) You _____ use _____ your _____ yacht.
b) Chimes _____ charm _____ church - es.
c) John's _____ grudge _____ jolts _____ Jill.
d) Age _____ chides _____ youth's _____ cheer.

STUDY

The Tongue and Hard-Palate Consonants (y, ch, j): Description and Execution

Y(y) is a voiced continuant and is articulated as follows:

1. The tip of the tongue is forward.
2. The middle of the tongue is raised toward the hard palate, with the sides of the tongue against the upper side teeth.
3. The voice is emitted over the tongue.

Ch(ch) consists of two voiceless consonants blended together and should be executed as follows:

1. The consonant *t* is articulated with the plosive omitted.
2. The tip of the tongue glides back from the gums over the front of the hard palate and drops quickly as the sibilant *sh* is emitted over it.

Remember that *t* is plosive and *sh* continuant. The two consonants must be blended together by a rapid movement of the tongue, so that *ch* will be clear and distinct.

J(j), sometimes spelled *g*, is a blend of two voiced consonants. Execute *j* as follows:

1. The consonant *d* is articulated with the plosive omitted.
2. The tip of the tongue glides back from the gums over the front of the hard palate and drops quickly as voiced *zh* is emitted over it.

Remember that *d* is plosive and *zh* continuant. Blend the two together smoothly and clearly.

Ch and *j* are called *blended consonants,* the only ones in English. All other consonants have single, unique sounds. *Ch* and *j* are to consonants what diphthongs are to vowels.

The Tongue and Hard-Palate Consonants (j, tʃ. dʒ): Common Faults and Corrections

Y(j): Y is sometimes a vowel sound. Memorize the following rules in order to recognize *y* as a consonant or vowel.

1. At the beginning of a syllable, *y* is a consonant.

    young   lawyer
    yield   barnyard

2. At all other times, *y* is a vowel.

    carry   marry
    merry   rhythm

When *y* occurs unstressed at the end of a word, it has the *IH* sound *(marry, merry).*

Caution: When words like *marry* and *merry* are rhymed with *EE* words *(me, be, she),* *y* has the *EE* sound.

When *y* follows a word ending with a consonant, the consonant is attached to *y* (*lo -vyou,* not *love - uh you,* and *leapyear,* not *leap - uh year*). Be particularly careful of the word *you* when it is preceded by a word ending with a consonant:

want you	is	*wan - tyou*	not	*one - chew*
did you	is	*did - uh you*	not	*di - djew*
bless you	is	*ble - syou*	not	*ble - shew*

Ch and *j*(tʃ, dʒ): *Ch* must be voiceless; *j* is voiced. Do not sing *chon* for *John, chust* for *just,* or *chest* for *jest.*

When *ch* or *j* occurs before a syllable or a word beginning with a vowel sound, it is attached to that syllable or vowel (*su-chis* for *such is,* and *pa-jate* for *page eight*).

When *ch* or *j* occurs before a consonant sound or a stop, avoid an extra *uh* sound (*tea - chme,* not *teach - uh me,* and *a - geto age,* not *age - uh to age - uh*).

When *ch* ends a word preceding another word beginning with *ch,* each *ch* must be sounded. The same rule applies to *j* (*such cheer* as *such/cheer,* not *su - cheer* or *such - uh cheer,* and *Judge James* as *Judge/James,* not *Juh -James* or *Judge - uh James*).

SONG INTERPRETATION AND MUSICIANSHIP
Sullivan, "When I Was a Lad"

This delightful "patter song" from *H.M.S. Pinafore,* one of Gilbert and Sullivan's most popular operettas, is a tongue twister. To articulate these words clearly requires painstaking work on all the principles of English diction. This song is an ideal staccato study and should be practiced on all vowels, with each note articulated separately.

Use this song as an articulation study by making up neutral syllables involving consonants. Place these consonants before vowels *(TAH)*, after vowels *(AHT)*, or both before and after vowels *(TAHT)*. Practice slowly at first and then accelerate.

The small cue notes in measure 7 indicate that in some stanza other than the first there is another syllable or word that must be included within the beat.

Practice speaking the words of the text in rhythm until you can do so clearly, then sing them.

Although this is a song for a male voice, females should sing it also for diction practice, substituting *lass* for *lad*, and *girl* for *boy* if desired.

The word *clerk* in this song should be given the British pronunciation *clark*. Other Gilbert and Sullivan patter songs you may wish to learn are:

"A Modern Major General" *(The Pirates of Penzance)*
"I've Got a Little List" *(The Mikado)*
"Said I to Myself" *(Iolanthe)*
"I Stole a Prince" *(The Gondoliers)*
"There Lived a King" *(The Gondoliers)*
"When I, Good Friends, Was Called to the Bar" *(Trial By Jury)*
"A Private Buffoon" *(The Yeoman of the Guard)*

Study also three more songs at the back of the book: Carl Engel's "Sea-Shell" (page 244), Reynaldo Hahn's "The Hour of Dreaming" (page 247), and the old English air "Drink to Me Only with Thine Eyes" (page 251).

Carl Engel was born in Germany in 1818 and died in England in 1882. He is remembered not only as a composer but also as an eminent writer about musical instruments. Because the tessitura of "Sea-Shell" is fairly high, low voices may find the song more comfortable in the key of E-flat. Sing with simplicity at the beginning, then follow the composer's instructions. A new term in this song is *ravvivando*, which means "quickening."

Reynaldo Hahn, though born in Venezuela, received his musical education in Paris. He wrote many kinds of music but is remembered primarily for his songs. "The Hour of Dreaming" ("L'Heure exquise") is a mood piece typical of French music written in the early part of the twentieth century. The voice and the piano, acting as partners, should seek to "paint a picture." Note that all three high F's are sung softly; lower male voices will probably wish to sing these pitches falsetto. Some may wish to transpose the key down to B-flat.

The lyrics of Ben Jonson have attracted many composers, including Arne, Auric, Britten, Delius, Elgar, Handel, Quilter, Richard Strauss, and Vaughan Williams. "Drink to Me Only with Thine Eyes" is Jonson's best-known poem. The song form is both three-part and strophic.

Sir Joseph Porter, the pompous, stuffy First Lord of the Admiralty, outlines the history of his rise to power and tells his listeners on H.M.S. "Pinafore" how they can all "be rulers of the Queen's Navee."

When I Was a Lad

Sir William S. Gilbert

Allegro non troppo

Sir Arthur S. Sullivan
(1842–1900)

Sir Joseph

When I was a lad I
As of - fice boy I
In serv - ing writs I
Of le - gal knowl - edge I ac -
I grew so rich that
Now lands - men all, who

served a term As of - fice boy to an at -
made such a mark That they gave me the post of a
made such a name That an ar - ti - cled clerk I
quired such a grip That they took me in - to the
I was sent By a pock - et bor - ough in - to the
ev - er you may be, If you want to rise to the

171

care - ful - ly, That___ now he is the ru - ler of the
hand___ so___ free, That___ now he is the ru - ler of the
well___ for___ me, That___ now he is the ru - ler of the
suit - ed___ me, That___ now he is the ru - ler of the
ward - ed___ he, By___ mak - ing him the ru - ler of the
nev - er go to sea, And you all___ may be ru - lers of the

Queen's Na - vee!
Queen's Na - vee!
Queen's Na - vee!
Queen's Na - vee!
Queen's Na - vee!
Queen's Na - vee!

After sixth stanza

Consonants Articulated with the Back of the Tongue

Webster's New World:	k, g, ŋ
American Heritage:	k, g, ng
International:	k, g, ŋ

WORDS WITH THE BACK-OF-TONGUE CONSONANTS

Read aloud slowly:

king	God	sing
kind	give	long
kick	grieve	bring
come	big	sung

Sing:

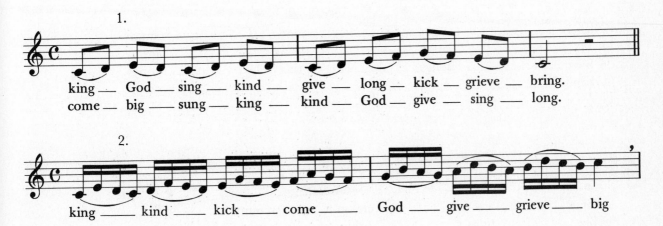

1.

king — God — sing — kind — give — long — kick — grieve — bring.
come — big — sung — king — kind — God — give — sing — long.

2.

king — kind — kick — come — God — give — grieve — big

sing —— long —— bring —— sung —— big —— grieve — give —— God.

3.

king —— kind —— kick —— come —— God —— give —— grieve —— big

sing —— long —— bring —— sung —— queen —grip —— ring —— cake.

4.

king —— king —— kick —— come —— God —— give —— grieve —— big.
sing —— long —— bring —— sung —— queen —— egg —— green —— wrong.

SENTENCES WITH THE BACK-OF-TONGUE CONSONANTS

Sing until all consonants are clearly executed:

1.

ⓐ Kings _____ can _____ crown _____ counts.
ⓑ Big _____ hugs _____ bring _____ grins.
ⓒ Sing _____ songs; _____ ring _____ gongs.
ⓓ Kind _____ goats _____ don't _____ kick.

2.

ⓐ Kings _____ can _____ crown _____ counts. _____
ⓑ Big _____ hugs _____ bring _____ grins. _____
ⓒ Sing _____ songs; _____ ring _____ gongs. _____
ⓓ Kind _____ goats _____ don't _____ kick. _____

STUDY
The Back-of-Tongue Consonants (k, g, ŋ, ng): Description and Execution

K(k)—sometimes spelled *c, ck, q,* or *ch*—is voiceless and stop-plosive. *K* is articulated as follows:

1. The tip of the tongue is forward.
2. The back of the tongue is raised against the soft palate.
3. The tongue is quickly lowered; breath is emitted over the tongue plosively.

G(g) is a voiced stop-plosive and is articulated as follows:

1. The tip of the tongue is forward.
2. The back of the tongue is raised against the soft palate.
3. The tongue is lowered quickly; the voice is emitted over the tongue plosively.

Ng(ŋ, ng) is a voiced, nasal continuant and should be articulated as follows:

1. The tip of the tongue is forward.
2. The back of the tongue is raised against the soft palate.
3. While this position is held, the voice is emitted through the nose.

The Back-of-Tongue Consonants (k, g, ŋ): Common Faults and Corrections

K and *g:* Many singers produce *h* rather than *k* because they do not make contact between the tongue and soft palate. Others voice the consonant, singing *g* rather than *k*. The reason for these mistakes is more psychological than physical. Singers are sometimes fearful of plosive, crisp sounds, particularly when singing *pp* or legato. In fact, however, crisply articulated *k*'s and hard *g*'s add to expressive singing.

K or *g* before a syllable or word beginning with a vowel is attached to the syllable or vowel *(wal - king, tri - gger)*.

K before a consonant is articulated just before the consonant. Do not add an *uh* sound (sing *dar - kwater*, not *dark - uh water*).

K before *t* or *ts* must not be omitted. To avoid this fault, practice the following:

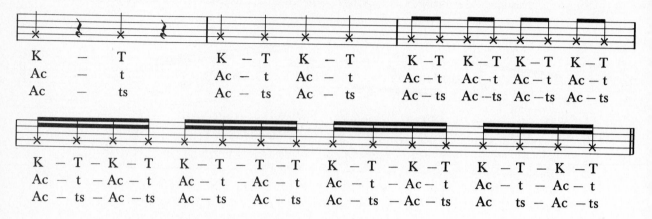

1. Whisper the sounds slowly.
2. Sing them, gradually increasing in speed.

When *k* ends a word preceding another word beginning with *k*, stop the first *k* without adding the plosive sound (called *implosion*) and explode the second *k* only (sing *speak quickly* as *spea / quickly*, not *speak - uh quickly*).

When *g* occurs before a consonant or stop, it is treated exactly like *b* (Lesson 13) and *d* (Lesson 15). That is, the weak vowel is appended; otherwise, *g* will not sound. Sing:

big   as   bi - guh

big   boy   as   bi - guh boy

There is one exception to this rule. When *g (b, d)* occurs before a word beginning with *w* or *y*, the weak vowel is not sounded; instead *g* is attached to *w* or *y* (sing *big year* as *bi - gyear*, *rob you* as *ro - byou*, and *dead wood* as *dea - dwood*).

SONG INTERPRETATION AND MUSICIANSHIP
Schubert, "Who Is Sylvia?"

Measure 5: Make a slight crescendo into measure 6. When singing the ♪., do not slide from *A* to *F*.

Measure 6: Make a slight stress on *Syl* with a fast ⟩ on *-via*.

Measures 7–8: Sing as in measures 5 and 6.

Measure 9: Starting with the last note in measure 8, make a long ⟨ to measure 10.

Measure 10: Crescendo slightly on the word *mend*, and decrescendo on *her*.

Measure 13: Observe the rest but do not take a breath.

Measures 16–17: Be careful of pitch.

Measure 21: Practice the ♪♪♪♪ figure until each note is on pitch and in correct rhythm.

Measures 23–34: Sing the octaves in tune. Do not stress the upper C (measure 23) as much as the upper D (measure 24).

Measure 25: Crescendo on the E, executing as gracefully as possible the ♫ figure on the fourth count.

Measure 29: Note the 𝄇, indicating a repeat from measure 5.

Three final songs have been included for your study. See first John Alden Carpenter's "The Sleep That Flits on Baby's Eyes" (page 254). Carpenter was an American composer, born in Chicago in 1876. Composing was more a hobby than a profession, since he was engaged in business most of his life. His music is characterized by delicacy and tender sentiment. This song is from the cycle *Gitanjali,* all of whose songs are settings of texts by the great Indian poet Rabindranath Tagore.

The second song, on page 257, is "I Love Thee," the best known of more than 130 songs composed by the Norwegian Edvard Grieg. Strive for a wide range of dynamic expression. Note the many ⟨ ⟩ combinations. This song is in strophic form. Seek to make measures 34–36 even more climactic than measures 16–18.

The third song is "Eldorado," written for this book by Wallace DePue (page 261). Both the piano and voice parts are very difficult and will present a challenge to the most advanced student.

"Eldorado" introduces a style of composition different from any other song in this book, the style called *serial* or *twelve-tone* composition. The songs that you have learned so far have all been in traditional major or minor keys. But twelve-tone music has no key. The twelve tones of the chromatic scale are arranged by the composer in any order that he chooses, without repeating any, so that no tone dominates the other eleven. This series of twelve tones, or *row,* is then used as the exclusive melodic and harmonic material of the composition. The row may be transposed to begin at any pitch level, may be inverted (turned over), retrograded (used backwards), or combined into chords. It may also be fragmented and used in pieces. The basic requirement is that all twelve tones of the row be used before any is repeated. The tones may be given any rhythmic or melodic shape, unless the rhythm itself is serialized.

In "Eldorado" the row is used differently for each of the four stanzas of Edgar Allen Poe's poem:

Stanza 1—the original row

Stanza 2—inversion of the original row (each interval turned over)

Stanza 3—retrograde of the original row (the row sung backwards)

Stanza 4—inversion of the retrograde (the row sung backwards but with each interval turned over)

Examples from the song itself should help to make this technique of composition clear. Pitches are placed under the word or syllable with which they occur. Numbers designate where the pitches occur in the row.

Original row

Verse I: Gayly bedight, a gallant knight, In sunshine and in shadow,

Pitches: C   G   A♭   E♭   D♭   F   F♯

Order: 1   2   3   4   5   6   7

Had journeyed long, Singing a song, In search of Eldorado.

Pitches:	D	B♭		A		B		E
Order:	8	9		10		11		12

Inversion of original row
Verse 2:   But he grew old—This knight so bold,—And o'er his heart a shadow

Pitches:	C		F		E	A		B	G	G♭	B♭
Order:	1		2		3	4		5	6	7	8

Fell as he found No spot of ground That looked like Eldorado.

Pitches:	D		E♭		D♭			A♭
Order:	9		10		11			12

Retrograde of original row
Verse 3:   And, as strength Failed him at length, he met a pilgrim shadow,

Pitches:	E	B	A		B♭		D	F♯	F	D♭
Order:	12	11	10		9		8	7	6	5

"Shadow," said he, "Where can it be—This land of Eldorado?"

Pitches:	E♭		A♭			G		C
Order:	4		3			2		1

Inversion of the retrograde
Verse 4:   "Over the mountains Of the Moon, Down the Valley of the Shadow,

Pitches:	E[1]	A		B	A♯		F♯	D[1]	E♭
Order:	12	11		10	9		8	7	6

Ride, boldly ride," The shade replied, "If you seek for Eldorado!"

Pitches:	G		F[1]		C	D♭			A♭
Order:	5		4		3	2			1

As you can see, twelve different pitches are used in each row, and no pitch is repeated. Thus no pitch is more important than any other; there is no key pitch, no tonal center.

Note that when an interval is inverted, it is simply "turned over." For example:

is an interval of a major third *up*. To invert that interval, we would have to write an interval of a major third *down* from G:

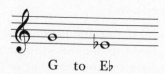

---

1. Octave displacement. The composer uses the same pitch but at a different octave.

If three intervals are inverted, the following would occur:

Similarly, all twelve tones of the chromatic scale, arranged in a prescribed order, may be inverted, as was done in stanzas 2 and 4 of "Eldorado." Careful study of the piano part will reveal that it too is constructed from the rows.[2]

To the student seeing and hearing twelve-tone technique for the first time, the system may seem arbitrary and contrived. But perhaps it is no more so than the familiar major-minor system.

Twelve-tone music is difficult to sing because it lies outside the experience of most students. But there is really no reason a diminished fifth (C to G-flat), for example, should be more difficult to sing than a major third. We simply must learn to hear such intervals.

Serial technique does not restrict the composer's imagination; rather it frees it from the restriction of keys by providing a substitute for traditional tonality.

Many of the leading composers of the twentieth century have used the twelve-tone system, including Arnold Schoenberg (who invented it), Igor Stravinsky, Alban Berg, Anton Webern, Aaron Copland, Gunther Schuller, and Roger Sessions. Listen to compositions in this style by these composers.

The verses for this song are taken from Act IV, Scene 2, of Shakespeare's play *Two Gentlemen of Verona*. Thurio, one of Sylvia's lovers, has written these lyrics and, together with a group of hired musicians, sings them to her.

---

2. A few tones have been altered.

Who Is Sylvia?

William Shakespeare

Franz Schubert

1. Who is Syl - via, What is
2. Is she kind, as she is
3. Then to Syl - via, let us

she That all our swains com - mend her?
fair? For beau - ty lives with kind - ness:
sing, That Syl - via is ex - cel - ing;

mir - ed _____ be, _____
hab - its _____ there, _____
gar - lands _____ bring, _____

And
That she
To be - ing
her

might ad - mir - ed _____ be.
help'd in - hab - its _____ there.
let us gar - lands _____ bring.

Song Appendix

Below in the Valley
Da unten im Tale

Johannes Brahms
(1833–1893)

Sanft bewegt (*Mildly moving*)

1. Be - low in the val - ley the wa - ter flows
2. You say that you love me, you say you'll be
1. Da un - ten im Ta - le läuft's Was - ser so
2. Sprichst all - weil von Lieb', sprichst all - weil von

p dolce

deep, And I love you so dear - ly, I hard - ly can
true, Yet a touch of a false - hood is in all you
trüb und i kann dir's nit sa - gen, i hab' di so
Treu', und a bis - se - le Falsch - heit is au wohl da -

dim.

speak.
do;
lieb.
bei!

Original key—E♭

* As a prelude, it would be well to use the interlude which begins at this point.

189

3. For the   time that   you loved   me my   thanks   I give
3. *Für die   Zeit,   wo   du g'liebt   mi hast,   dank   i dir*

thee,___   With a   hope that   an - o -ther love   tru -   er may
schön,___   und i   wünsch' dass   dir's an-ders-wo   bes -   ser mag

be.
gehn.

My Lovely Celia

George Monro
(b? —d. 1731)

With expression

love - ly —— Ce - lia, heav'n - ly —— fair, As

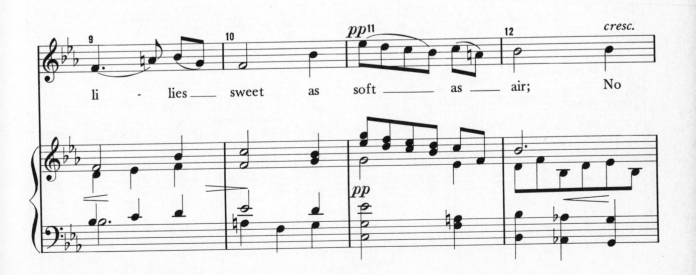

li - lies —— sweet as soft —— as —— air; No

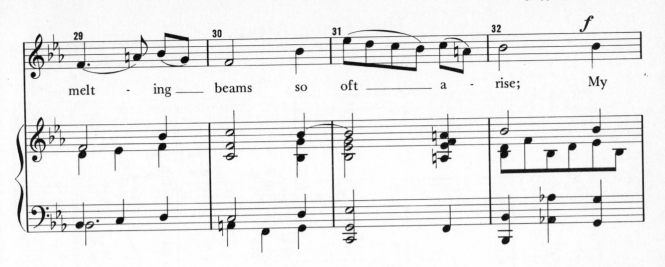

melt - ing __ beams so oft __ a - rise; My

heart's __ en - chant - ed with __ thy __ charms, O,

take __ me, __ dy - ing, __ to __ your arms. __
(dy - ing)

He's Gone Away

Southern Mountain Song
Arr. by Wallace De Pue

way, Look a - way, Look a - way o - ver yon - dro. *Fine*

slightly faster

1. Oh who — will tie your shoe? And who — will glove your
2. My pap - py will tie my shoe, And mam - my will glove my

(D.S. after verse 2)

hand? And who will kiss your ru - by lips when I am gone?
hand, And you will kiss my ru - by lips when you come home.

The Lass with the Delicate Air

Michael Arne

Mol - ly who — lived at the foot — of — the — hill, Whose
eve - ning last — May, as I trav - ersed — the — grove, In

fame — ev'ry — la - dy with en - vy doth fill, Of
thought - less — re - tire - ment, not dream - ing of love, I

call — her — the — lass — with — the — del - i - cate air.
real - ly — she — had — a — most — del - i - cate air.

colla voce
poco rit.

f a tempo

First time D.C.

3. By a mur - mur - ing — brook, on a green moss - y — knoll, A
4. A — thou - sand times — o'er I've re - peat - ed — my — suit, But

- i-cate air, — With — rap - ture — to — gaze — on — her — del - i - cate —

- i-cate air, — How to

rit. colla voce   _a tempo_
                     _pp_   _poco rit._

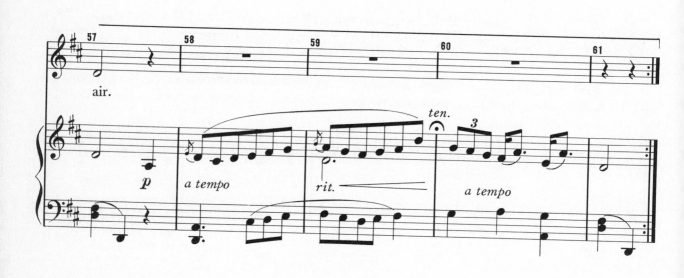

air.

_p_   _a tempo_   _rit._   _a tempo_

win — the — dear — lass — with — the — del - i - cate   air.

colla voce   _rit._   _p a tempo_

Dido's Lament

Nahum Tate

Henry Purcell
(1659–1695)

When I am laid, ___ am laid ___ in earth, may my

wrongs ___ cre - ate no trou - ble, no trou - ble in thy

ah! __ for __ get __ my fate. Re - mem - ber me, but

ah! _____ for - get my __ fate.

* Low voices may sing the small notes here.

O Mistress Mine

William Shakespeare

Roger Quilter
(1877—1953)

Ave Maria
Mary, We Hail Thee

Sir Walter Scott

Franz Schubert
(1797–1828)

1. *Training text:* Ma - ry we hail _____
2. *Latin text:* *1. A - ve Ma - ri -
   2. A - ve Ma - ri -

* When singing the Latin text, sing stanzas 1 and 2 and repeat stanza 1 as a third verse.

Passing By

Robert Herrick

Edward Purcell
(1689–1740)

1. There is a la - dy
2. Her ges-tures, mo - tions,

sweet and kind, was nev - er face so pleased my mind; I
and her smiles, Her wit, her voice my heart __ be - guiles, Be -

did __ but see her pass - ing by, And yet I love her
guiles __ my heart, I know not why, And yet I love her

Little Lamb

William Blake

Wallace De Pue

Evening Fair
Beau soir

Claude Debussy
(1862–1918)

Andante, ma non troppo

Piano

When from the set - ting sun ev - 'ry
Lorsque au so - leil cou - chant les ri -

brook - let is gleam - ing, When a beau - ti - ful
viè - res sont ro - ses, Et qu'un tiè - de fris -

An a - vow   to en - gage the ut - ter joy of
Un con - seil   de goû - ter le char - me d'être au

be - - ing,   In this day   of my   youth, and while the eve - ning's
mon - - de,   Ce - pen-dant   qu'on est   jeune et que le soir est

fair,_____   For   we shall all de - part,
beau,_____   Car   nous nous en al - lons,

The Vagabond

Robert Louis Stevenson

Ralph Vaughan Williams
(1872–1958)

Allegro moderato
(alla marcia)

p ma sempre marcato

sempre pesante il basso

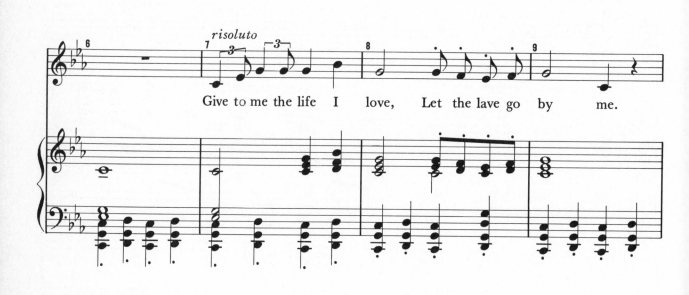

risoluto

Give to me the life I love, Let the lave go by me.

Give the jol - ly heaven a - bove, And the by - way nigh me.

Bed in the bush with stars to see, Bread I dip in the ri - - ver, There's the life for a man like me, There's the life for ev - er.

colla voce

Let the blow fall soon or late, Let what will be o'er me;

O Lord Most Holy

Panis angelicus

César Franck
(1822–1890)

Lullaby

Wallace De Pue

fly - ing through the night ___ to find, Hid-den in slum - ber,

vi - sions of ___ de - light. Ice - cream moun-tains and so ___ - da foun-tains and

can - dy or-chards you'll see Choc-o-late makers and ap-ple pie bak-ers are

a lttle faster

faster

Cradle Song
Wiegenlied

Johannes Brahms
(1833-1897)

Zart bewegt
Dolce, con moto

Go to bed now, good night, with ___ ros - es be - dight, ___ All ___ bun - dled with ___ bows, sleep ___ un - der the clothes. When the morn - ing doth break, please the Lord, thou shalt wake, When the morn - ing doth break, please the Lord, thou shalt wake!

Gu - ten A - bend, gut' Nacht, mit ___ Ro - sen be - dacht, ___ mit Näg - lein be - steckt, schlüpf' un - ter die Deck: Mor - gen früh, wenn Gott will, wirst du wie - der ge - weckt, mor - gen früh, wenn Gott will, wirst du wie - der ge - weckt!

Go to bed now, good night, fond an - gels de - light, — In — dreams thou wilt — see a — green — Christ-mas tree. Go to sleep, close your eyes, thou wilt see Par - a - dise! Go to sleep, close your eyes, thou wilt see Par - a - dise!

Gu - ten A - bend, gut' Nacht, von Eng - lein be - wacht, — die — zei - gen im — Traum dir — Christ-kind - leins Baum: Schlaf' nun se - lig und süss, schau' im Traum's Pa - ra - dies! schlaf' nun se - lig und süss, schau' im Traum's Pa - ra - dies!

Silent Noon

Dante Gabriel Rossetti

Ralph Vaughan Williams

Your hands lie o - pen in the long fresh grass, The fin - ger - points look through like ros - y blooms: Your eyes smile

peace.   The pas-ture gleams and glooms 'Neath bil - low-ing

mf   *cresc.*

skies   that   scat - ter   and a - mass. ____

f

Poco più mosso

pp

p   All   round   our   nest,   far   as   the   eye   can   pass,   Are

Oh, clasp we to our hearts, for____ death - less dower, This close-com - pan - ioned in - ar - tic - u-late hour, When two - fold si - lence was the song, _____ the ____ song of love.

O Rest in the Lord

Psalm XXXVII

Felix Mendelssohn
(1809–1847)

Sea-Shell

Amy Lowell

Carl Engel
(1883–1944)

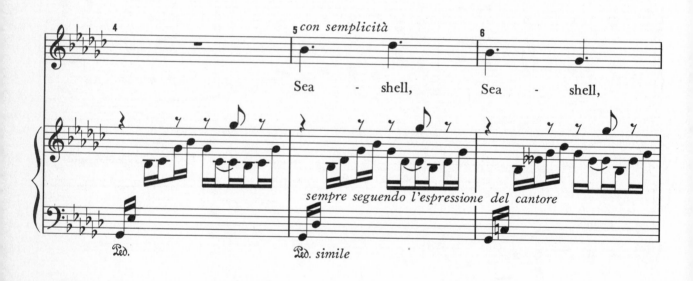

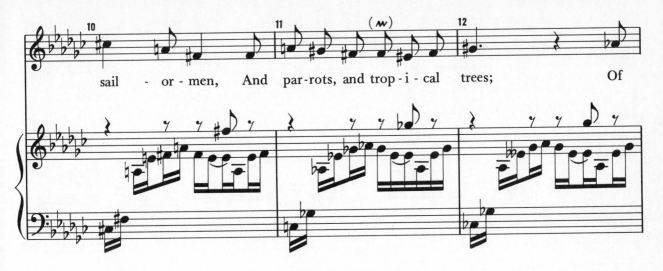

sail - or - men, And par-rots, and trop - i - cal trees; Of

is - lands lost in the Span - ish Main, Which no man ev - er may

find a - gain, Of fish - es and cor - als un - der the waves, And

sea - hors - es sta - bled in great green caves. Oh, Sea - shell,

Sea - shell, Sing of the things you know_____ so

well. _____

The Hour of Dreaming

L'Heure exquise

Reynaldo Hahn
(1875–1947)

show, Where winds are weep - ing: Oh love!_____ art
noir Où le vent pleu - re..... Rê - vons!_____ c'est

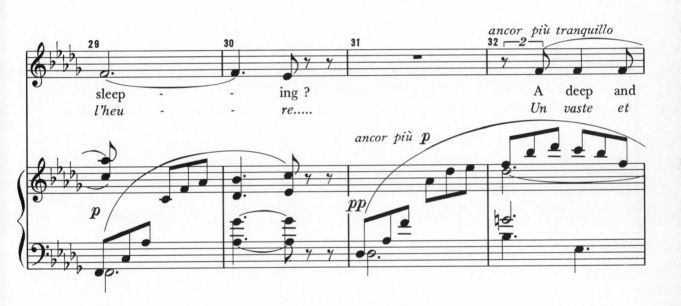

sleep - - ing? A deep and
l'heu - - re..... Un vaste et

ten - der Calm now lies O'er___ all things un - der Yon arch - ing
ten - dre A-pai-se - ment Sem - ble des - cen - dre Du fir - ma -

skies   Where stars   are   gleam - ing:
ment   Que l'astre   i - ri - se.....

Oh   hour   of   dream - - - - ing!
C'est   l'heu - re ex - qui - - - se.

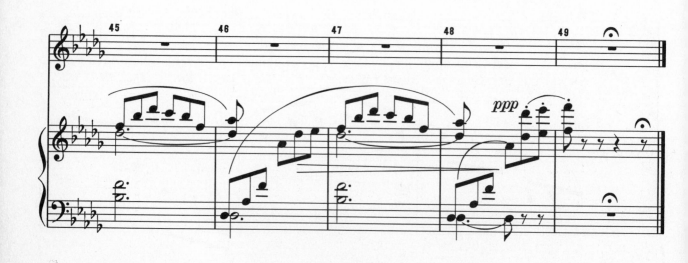

Drink to Me Only with Thine Eyes

Ben Jonson
(1573-1637)

Old English Air
(Date uncertain)

Very smoothly, and rather slow

Drink to me on - ly with thine eyes, And I will pledge with mine,

Or leave a kiss with - in the cup, And I'll not ask for wine; The

thirst that from the soul doth rise, Doth ask a drink di - vine,

But might I of Jove's nec - tar sip, I would not change for

thine!

I sent thee late a ros - y wreath, Not so much hon'-ring thee

The Sleep That Flits on Baby's Eyes

Rabindranath Tagore

John Alden Carpenter
(1876–1951)

The sleep that flits__ on ba-by's eyes, does an-y-bod-y know__ from where it comes?

I Love Thee

Ich liebe dich

Edvard Grieg
(1843–1907)

I love thee more than an- y earth-ly crea - ture, I love thee,dear, I
Ich lie - be dich wie nichts auf die -ser Er - den, ich lie - be dich, ich

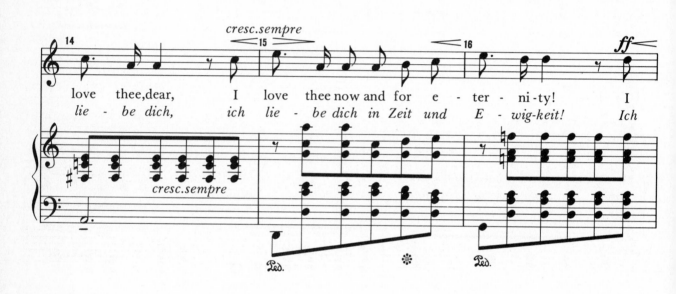

love thee,dear, I love thee now and for e - ter - ni -ty! I
lie - be dich, ich lie - be dich in Zeit und E - wig-keit! Ich

love thee now and for e - ter - ni -ty!
lie - be dich in Zeit und E - wig-keit!

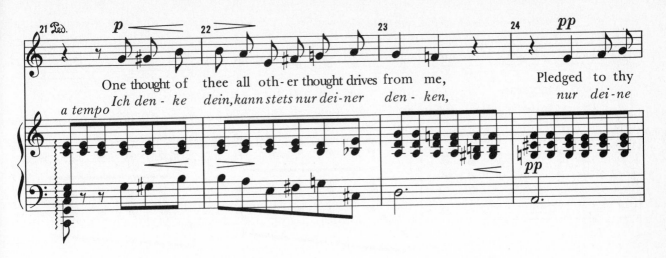

One thought of thee all oth-er thought drives from me, Pledged to thy
Ich den - ke dein, kann stets nur dei-ner den - ken, *nur dei-ne*

good a-lone this heart shall be; For to what -
Glück ist die - ses Herz ge-weiht; *wie Gott auch*

ev - er fate God's will may doom me, I love thee, dear, I
mag des Le - bens Schick-sal len - ken, *ich lie - be dich,* *ich*

love thee, dear,   I   love thee now and for   e - ter - ni-ty,   I
lie - be dich,   ich   lie - be dich in Zeit und   E - wig-keit!   Ich

love thee now and for e - ter - ni-ty!
lie - be dich in Zeit und E- wig-keit!

Eldorado

Edgar Allan Poe

Wallace De Pue

Gai-ly be-dight, A gal-lant knight, In sun-shine and in shad-ow, ___ Had jour-neyed long, Sing-ing a song, In search ___ of El-do-ra-do. ___

Selected, Graded, and Categorized List of Songs

Grades: **A—advanced**
   B—medium
   C—fairly easy

Grade is an attempt to indicate technical difficulty only and is at best a nebulous procedure. It is not intended as an index of the musical and dramatic insight required for each song, but rather only as a general guide for technical difficulty. Collections are not graded. A key to publishers is provided on page 276. Certain songs in each category may be sung by other voices. Titles are listed as they appear on the printed copies; thus a song may be listed more than once under different titles.

Soprano
(Specify high key when ordering.)

Grade A

Bach/Deis, "Mein glaubiges Herze" ("My Heart Ever Faithful")	GS
Bach/LaForge, "Now the Sheep Secure Are Grazing"	CF
Barber, "Must the Winter Come So Soon" (from *Vanessa*), *Contemporary Art Songs* (single)	GS
Bergsma, "Doll's Boys Asleep"	CF
Bernstein, "A Simple Song" (from *Mass*)	GS
Bononcini, "Per la gloria d'adorarvi," *24 Italian Songs and Arias*	GS
Bridge, "Love Went A-Riding"	BH
Copland, "Laurie's Song" (from *The Tender Land*)	BH
Davis, "Nancy Hanks"	GAL/ECS
Debussy, "Beau soir" ("Evening Fair"), *56 Songs You Like to Sing*	GS

Delibes, "Les filles de Cadiz" ("The Maids
of Cadiz")   GS

Dello Joio, "All Things Leave Me"   CF

Duke, "The Mountains Are Dancing"   CF

Giannini, "Tell Me, Oh Blue, Blue Sky" COL/BEL

Gluck, "O del mio dolce ardor"   GS

Grieg, "Solveig's Song," *56 Songs You Like
to Sing* (single)   GS

Hageman, "Do Not Go, My Love," *56 Songs
You Like to Sing* (single)   GS

Hahn, "Were My Song with Wings Provided,"
56 Songs You Like to Sing   GS

Handel, "Care selve"   CF

Handel, "Come unto Me"   GS

Handel, "I Know That My Redeemer
Liveth" (from *Messiah*)   GS

Handel, "Oh, Had I Jubal's Lyre," *45 Arias from
Operas and Oratorios*, Vol. II (single)   GS

Handel, "Rejoice Greatly" (from *Messiah*)
(in complete score only)   GS

Handel, "Sempre dolce ed amorose"   GS

Haydn, "With Verdure Clad"   GS

Head, "A Green Cornfield," *A Heritage of 20th
Century British Song*, Vol. II   BH

Head, "The Piper"   BH

Head, "The Singer," *Imperial Edition* (single) BH

Kingsley, "The Green Dog," *20th Century
Art Songs*   GS

Lekberg, "O Come Let Us Sing unto the
Lord"   GAL/ECS

Marcello, "Il mio bel foco," *Anthology of Italian
Song*, Vol. I   GS

Mayerl, "These Precious Things"   BH

Mendelssohn, "Hear Ye Israel"   GS

Menotti, "The Black Swan" (from *The
Medium*), *20th Century Art Songs* (single)   GS

Mozart, "Alleluia"   GS

Mozart, "Deh vieni, non tarder" (from *Marriage
of Figaro*), *Operatic Anthology*, Vol. II (single) GS

Pergolesi, "Se tu m'ami," *24 Italian
Songs and Arias*   GS

Puccini, "O mio babbino caro" (from
Gianni Schicchi)   GS

Puccini, "Quando m'en vo" (Musetta's Waltz
Song) (from *La Bohème*)   GS

Scarlatti, "Se florindo e fedele," *24 Italian Songs
and Arias*   GS

Scarlatti, "Le violette," *24 Italian Songs and Arias* GS

Spross, "Let All My Life Be Music"   TP

Strauss, "Zueignung" ("To You"), *56 Songs You
Like to Sing*   GS

Thiman, "I Love All Graceful Things,"
Contemporary Art Songs   GS

Tyson, "Sea Moods," *Songs by 22 Americans*   GS

Verdi, "Caro nome" (from *Rigoletto*)   GS

Watts, "The Little Shepherd's Song"   BEL

Grade B

Barber, "Sure on This Shining Night"   GS

Bishop, "Lo, Hear the Gentle Lark"   GS

Brahms, "A Thought Like Music"   TP

Campbell/Tipton, "Spirit Flower"   GS

Carpenter, "The Sleep That Flits on
Baby's Eyes"   GS

Charles, "Let My Song Fill Your Heart"   GS

Davis, "The Pitcher"   GAL/ECS

Delibes, "Bonjour, Suzon"   CF

Diamond, "Brigid's Song"   TP

Dougherty, "The K'e," *20th Century Art Songs* GS

Dunhill, "To the Queen of Heaven,"
Contemporary Art Songs   GS

Edmunds, "Billy Boy"   CF

Elwell, "All Foxes"   GS

Elwell, "The Glittering Grief"   GS

Elwell, "Phoenix Afire"   GS

Gibbs, "Nod," *A Heritage of 20th Century
British Song*, Vol. II   BH

Gounod, "O Divine Redeemer"   CF

Grieg, "My Johann"   GS

Hageman, "Fear Not the Night"   CF

Handel, "Angels Ever Bright and Fair,"
45 Arias from Operas and Oratorios, Vol. II
(single-GS)   INT

Handel, "Come Unto Him" (from *Messiah*)
(single)   GS

Handel, "Come and Trip It"   BH

Handel, "Oh, Had I Jubal's Lyre"   GS

Handel, "Verdant Meadows"   WB

Haydn, "She Never Told Her Love"   GS

Malotte, "The Beatitudes"   GS

Malotte, "The Twenty-Third Psalm"   GS

Mendelssohn, "On Wings of Song,"
The Young Singer (single)   CF

Monroe, "Hopak"   GS

Moores, "Red, Rosey Bush," *Four Traditional
American Songs*   BR/ABI

Mozart, "Das Veilchen" ("The Violet"),
56 Songs You Like to Sing   GS

Naginski, "The Pasture," *Songs by
22 Americans* (single)   GS

Purcell, "Man Is for the Woman Made"   BH

Rachmaninoff, "Lilacs," *56 Songs You
Like to Sing*   GS

Rowley, "The Prophecy," *Cycle of Three Mystical Songs* — BH

Rowley, "Three Jolly Shepherds," *Cycle of Three Mystical Songs* — BH

Schubert, "Hark, Hark the Lark" — TP

Strauss, "Devotion" — TP

Strauss, "Tomorrow" — TP

Wolf, "Verborgenheit" — TP

Yon, "O Faithful Cross" — JF

Grade C

Bach/Prout, "In Faith I Quiet Wait" — GAL

Barber, "The Daisies," *Collected Songs* (single) — GS

Beethoven, "I Love Thee," *56 Songs You Like to Sing* (single) — GS

Brahms, "Wiegenlied" ("Cradle Song") — GS

Brahms, "Sandmännchen" — GS

Carey, "Pastoral," *The Young Singer* — CF

Dawson, "Jesus Walked This Lonesome Valley" — WB

Dungan, "Where Is My Heart?" — BEL

Engel, "Sea-Shell," *50 Art Songs from the Modern Repertoire* — GS

Grieg, "A Swan," *The Young Singer* — CF

Head, "A Slumber Song of the Madonna" — BH

Humperdinck, "Evening Prayer" (from *Hansel and Gretel*) — CF

MacDowell, "Thy Beaming Eyes" — CF

Mozart, "Cradle Song" — GS

Niles, "The Black Oak Tree" — CF

Old English, "When Love Is Kind," *The Young Singer* — CF

Purcell, "Man Is for the Woman Made" — BH

Purcell, "Nymphs and Shepherds" — OX

Schubert, "Thou Art Repose" — GS

Thompson, "My Master Hath a Garden" — ECS

Thompson, "Velvet Shoes" — ECS

Thiman, "Thou Wilt Keep Him in Perfect Peace" — HWG

Mezzo-Soprano

(Specify medium key when ordering)

Grade A

Bach/Kramer, "Schafe Können sicher weiden" ("Sheep May Safely Graze") — GAL/ECS

Bantock, "A Feast of Lanterns" — NOV

Barber, "Must the Winter Come So Soon" (from *Vanessa*), *Contemporary Art Songs* — GS

Bononcini, "Per la gloria d'adorarvi," *24 Italian Songs and Arias* — GS

Bowling, "He Shall Be Like a Tree" — CF

Bridge, "Love Went A-Riding" — BH

Carpenter, "When I Bring to You Colored Toys" — GS

Charles, "Over the Land Is April" — WIL

Davis, "I Have a Fawn" — GAL/ECS

Dvořák, "I Will Sing New Songs of Gladness" — AMP

Gaul, "Eye Hath Not Seen" — GS

Gluck, "Che faro senza Euridice" (from *Orfeo*) — GS

Guion, "At the Cry of the First Bird" — GS

Hageman, "At the Well" — GS

Handel, "Care selve" — CF

Handel, "Lord, to Thee Each Night and Day" — GAL

Mendelssohn, "O for the Wings of a Dove" — GS

Moore, "Old Song" — CF

Mozart, "Voi che sapete" (from *The Marriage of Figaro*), *Operatic Anthology*, Vol. II (single) — GS

Olmstead, "Thy Sweet Singing" — GS

Pergolesi, "Se tu m'ami," *24 Italian Songs and Arias* — GS

Ponchielli, "Voce di donna" (from *La Gioconda*), *Operatic Anthology*, Vol. II (single) — GS

Rorem, "Lullaby of the Woman on the Mountain" — BH

Scarlatti, "Se florindo e fedele," *24 Italian Songs and Arias* — GS

Schubert, "Ständchen" ("Serenade") — GS

Schubert, "An die Musik" ("To Music") — OX

Spross, "Let All My Life Be Music" — TP

Thomas, "Connais-tu le pays?" ("Knowest Thou Not That Fair Land?") (from *Mignon*), *Operatic Anthology*, Vol. II (single) — GS

Ware, "This Day Is Mine" — BMC

Watts, "The Little Shepherd's Song" — BEL

Whelpley, "The Nightingale Has a Lyre of Gold" — BMC

Grade B

Bantock, "Silent Strings" — BH

Brahms, "Sapphische Ode" ("Sapphic Ode"), *56 Songs You Like to Sing* (single) — GS

Charles, "Let My Song Fill Your Heart" — GS

Charles, "Over the Land Is April" — WIL

Crist, "April Rain" — CF

Curran, "Gratitude" — GS

Davis, K. K., "I Have a Fawn" — GAL

Delibes, "Passepied" — GS

Diers, "Stopping by Woods on a Snowy Evening" — GAL/ECS

Dvořák, "Lord, Thou Art My Refuge,"
Biblical Songs   AMP

Edmonds, "I Know My Love"   CF

Finzi, "Fear No More the Heat o' the Sun,"
A Heritage of 20th Century British Song,
Vol. II   BH

German, "Who'll Buy My Lavender?"   WIL

Gibbs, "Silver," *A Heritage of 20th Century
British Song,* Vol. II   BH

Handel, "He Shall Feed His Flock" (from
Messiah) (single)   GS

Haydn, "My Mother Bids Me Bind My Hair,"
The Young Singer   CF

or *56 Songs You Like to Sing* (single)   GS

Hunt, "Only the Children Know"   BEL

Liadoff, "Musical Snuff Box"   GS

Mendelssohn, "On Wings of Song"   GS

Naginski, "The Pasture," *Songs by 22 Americans*   GS

Niles, "Wayfaring Stranger"   GS

Quilter, "Music When Soft Voices Die"   BH

Roberton, "All in the April Evening,"
20th Century Art Songs   GS

Rorem, "Rain in Spring"   BH

Scott, "Lullaby"   NOV

Thiman, "The God of Love
My Shepherd Is"   HWG

Thomson, "My Shepherd Will Supply My
Need"   BEL

Van de Water, "The Publican"   TP

Weaver, "Moon-Marketing"   GS

MacGimsey, "Sweet Little Jesus Boy"   CF

Moores, "Cripple Creek," *Four Traditional
American Songs*   BR/ABI

Moores, "Single Girl," *Four Traditional
American Songs*   BR/ABI

Niles, "The Black Dress," *The Songs of
John Jacob Niles*   GS

Old English, "When Love Is Kind,"
The Young Singer   CF

Peterkin, "I Heard a Piper Piping"   OX

Pinkham, D., "Elegy"   ECS

Raynor, "An Old Lullaby"   OX

Reichardt, "When the Roses Bloom,"
The Young Singer   CF

Scott, "Think on Me"   WIL

Shaw, C., "Since First I Saw Your Face"   CF

Sinding, "Sylvelin," *56 Songs You Like to Sing*   GS

Speaks, "Morning"   GS

Taylor, D., "La petite robe"   JF

Thompson, R., "My Master Hath a Garden"   ECS

Thompson, R., "Velvet Shoes"   ECS

Thomson, V., "My Shepherd Will Supply
My Need"   HWG

Van de Water, "The Penitent"   TP

Vaughan Williams, "Linden Lea"   BH

Weill, "Lonesome Dove," *20th Century Art Songs*   GS

Grade C

Barber, "The Daisies"   GS

Bernstein, "It Must Be Me," *20th Century
Art Songs*   GS

Boyce-Taylor, "What Beauties Doth My
Nymph Disclose"   OX

Chanler, "The Lamb"   AMP

Coates, "Bird Songs at Eventide"   CHAP

Copland, "Simple Gifts"   BH

Dolmetsch, "Have You Seen But a White
Lily Grow"   GS

Dougherty, "The Minor Bird," *20th Century
Art Songs* (single)   GS

Edmunds, "Fare You Well"   CF

Fauré, "Adieu"   GS

Franz, "Für Musik" ("For Music"),
The Young Singer   CF

Godard, "Florian's Song"   GS

Grieg, "A Swan," *The Young Singer*   CF

Haydn, "She Never Told Her Love"   GS

Alto

(Specify low key when ordering)

Grade A

Bach/Kramer, "Schafe können sicher weiden"
("Sheep May Safely Graze")   GAL/ECS

Bantock, "A Feast of Lanterns"   GAL

Bantock, "Silent Strings"   BH

Barber, "I Hear an Army"   GS

Berger, "Heart"   BRO

Berger, "Lonely People"   BRO

Bizet, "Habañera" (*Carmen*)   GS

Bridge, "Love Went A-Riding"   BH

Davis, K., "The Deaf Old Woman"   GAL

Dougherty, "Loveliest of Trees"   BH

Dunn, "The Bitterness of Love"   JF

Dvořák, "God Is My Shepherd," *Biblical Songs*   GS

Dvořák, "Hear My Prayer, O Lord,"
Biblical Songs   GS

Gluck, "O del mio dolce ardor"   GS

Grieg, "With a Water Lily"   GS

Hageman, "Miranda" — GAL
Hageman, "Music I Heard with You" — GAL/ECS
Hahn, "Were My Song with Wings Provided," *French Art Songs* — TP
Handel, "He Was Despised" (from *Messiah*) — GS
Handel, "O Thou That Tellest Good Tidings" (from *Messiah*) — GS
Homer, "Sheep and Lambs" — GS
Kramer, "Swans" — BEL
Leoncavallo, "Mattinata," *Great Art Songs of Three Centuries* — GS
Loughborough, "How Lovely Is the Hand of God" — TP
Moore, "Old Song," *Contemporary Songs in English* (single) — CF
Purcell, "I Attempt from Love's Sickness to Fly" — GS
Scarlatti, "Le violette" ("The Violet"), *24 Italian Songs and Arias* — GS
Schubert, "Der Tod und das Mädchen" ("Death and the Maiden"), *24 Favorite Songs* — GS
Schumann, "The Lotus Flower" — GS
Scott, "Lullaby" — GAL
Strauss, "Serenade" — GS
Thomas, "Connais-tu le pays?" ("Knowest Thou Not the Land?") (from *Mignon*), *Operatic Anthology*, Vol. II — GS
Tyson, "Sea Moods," *Songs by 22 Americans* — GS

Grade B

Berger, "Heart," *Four Songs* — BRO
Bishop, "Love Has Eyes," *The Young Singer* — CF
Bohm, "Calm as the Night" — CF, GS
Britten, "Ash Grove," *Folk Songs of the British Isles,* Vol. I — BH
Davis, "He's Gone Away" — GAL/ECS
Dunhill, "The Cloths of Heaven" — GAL
Dvořák/Spaeth, "Songs My Mother Taught Me," *55 Art Songs* — SU
Elgar, "Where Corals Lie" — NOV
Finzi, "Come Away, Come Away, Death," *A Heritage of 20th Century British Song,* Vol. II — BH
Finzi, "Fear No More the Heat o' the Sun," *A Heritage of 20th Century British Song,* Vol. II — BH
Gretchaninoff, "Slumber Song," *Singable Songs for Studio and Recital* — TP
Grieg, "With a Water Lily," *Pathways of Song,* Vol. III — WB
Handel, "He Shall Feed His Flock" (from *Messiah*) (single) — GS

Harty, "My Pagan Love" — BH
Horn, "I've Been Roaming" — TP
Ives, "Night Song" — SMP
Loughborough, "How Lovely is the Hand of God," *Singable Songs for Studio and Recital* — TP
Morgan, "Clorinda" — BH
Naginski, "The Pasture," *Songs by 22 Americans* — GS
Mendelssohn, "O Rest in the Lord" (from *Elijah*), *56 Songs You Like to Sing* (single) — GS
Owens, "Laudamus" — BMC
Ronald, "O Lovely Night" — BH
Rorem, "Rain in Spring" — BH
Schubert, "An die Musik" ("To Music"), *Imperial Edition* — BH
Scott, "Lullaby" — NOV
Sjöberg, "Visions" — GAL
Tchaikovsky, "None But the Lonely Heart" — GS
Tosti, "The Last Song" — BEL
Tyson, "Sea Moods" — GS
Whelpley, "The Nightingale Has a Lyre of Gold" — BMC

Grade C

Barber, "The Daisies" — GS
Berger, "Lonely People," *Four Songs* — BRO
Bernstein, L., "It Must Be Me" — GS
Britten, "Sally Gardens," *Folk Songs of the British Isles,* Vol. I — BH
Charles, "Sweet Song of Long Ago" — GS
Davis, "The Soldier" — GAL/ECS
Dodge, M. & J., "Gossiping" — WIL
Duke, "In the Fields" — CF
Dougherty, "The Minor Bird" — GS
Ferrari, "The Mirror" — EBM
Holst, "The Heart Worships" — GAL/ECS
Martin, "Crown of the Year" — BH
Niles, "Go 'Way from My Window" — GS
Niles, "The Lass from the Low Countree," *The Songs of John Jacob Niles* (single) — GS
Quilter, "Fuschia Tree" — BH
Ravel, "Chanson espagnole," *50 Art Songs from the Modern Repertoire* — GS
Sgambati, "Separazione" ("Separation"), *Great Art Songs of Three Centuries* — GS
Stanford, "Soft Day" — GAL
Thiman, "God of Love My Shepherd Is" — HWG
Vaughan Williams, "Linden Lea" — BH
Weill, "The Lonesome Dove" — GS

Tenor
(Specify high key when ordering)

Grade A

Barber, "Sure on This Shining Night"   GS
Bassett, "Take Joy Home"   GS
Bernstein, "A Simple Song" (from *Mass*)   GS
Brahms, "The May Night"   GS
Bridge, "Love Went A-Riding"   BH
Carissimi, "Vittoria, Vittoria Mio Core,"
  24 Italian Songs and Arias   GS
Charles, "My Lady Walks in Loveliness"   GS
Donaudy, "O del mio amato ben"   GS
Donaudy, "Spirate"   GS
Donaudy, "Vaghissima sembianza"   GS
Fauré, "Après un reve," *50 Art Songs from
  the Modern Repertoire* (single)   GS
Fauré, "En priere" ("In Prayer"), *50 Art Songs
  from the Modern Repertoire*   GS
Giannini, "Tell Me, Oh Blue, Blue Sky"   COL/BEL
Grieg, "A Swan"   GS
Guion, "At the Cry of the First Bird"   GS
Guion, "I Talked to God Last Night"   GS
Hageman, "Do Not Go My Love," *56 Songs You
  Like to Sing* (single)   GS
Hahn, "Were My Song with Wings Provided,"
  56 Songs You Like to Sing   GS
Handel, "Every Valley" (from *Messiah*)   GS
Handel, "They Rebuke," "Behold and See"
  (from *Messiah*)   GS
Handel, "Where'er You Walk," *The Young
  Singer* (single)   CF
Harker, "How Beautiful Upon the Mountains"   GS
Ireland, "Sea Fever"   GAL
Laddle, "How Lovely Are Thy Dwellings"   BH
Leoncavallo, "Mattinata," *Great Art Songs of
  Three Centuries*   GS
Mendelssohn, "Then Shall the Righteous
  Shine" (from *Elijah*)   GS
Mendelssohn, "If With All Your Hearts"
  (from *Elijah*) (single)   GS
Menotti, "The Hero," *20th Century Art Songs*   GS
Noble, "Grieve Not the Holy Spirit"   HWG
O'Hara, "Bright Is the Ring of Words"   CF
Pergolesi, "Nina," *24 Italian Songs and Arias*   GS
Purcell, "I'll Sail upon the Dog-Star"   INT
Quilter, "Fear No More the Heat o' the Sun,"
  Five Shakespeare Songs, 2nd Set   BH
Quilter, "O Mistress Mine," *Three Shakespeare
  Songs* (single)   BH

Rachmaninoff, "In the Silence of the Night"   GS
Respighi, "Nebbie" ("Mists"), *50 Art Songs
  from the Modern Repertoire*   GS
Rogers, "Great Peace Have They"   GS
Sacco, "Brother Will, Brother John"   GS
Thiman, "I Love All Graceful Things,"
  Contemporary Art Songs   GS
Tchaikovsky, "The Pilgrim's Song," *The
  Young Singer* (single-GS)   CF
Walton, "Under the Greenwood Tree"   BH
Wood, "A Bird Sang in the Rain"   CHAP
Young-Wilson, "Phyllis Has Such a
  Charming Grace"   BH

Grade B

Bach-LaForge, "Now the Sheep Secure
  are Grazing"   CF
Ball, "Who Knows"   WB
Bantock, "Silent Strings"   BH
Barber, "The Daisies," *Collected Songs* (single)   GS
Bitgood, "Give Me Faith"   HWG
Bowles, "Heavenly Grass," *Contemporary Art
  Song: Blue Mountain Ballads* (single)   GS
Britten, "The Ash Grove," *Folk Songs of the
  British Isles*, Vol. I (single)   BH
Britten, "The Ploughboy," *Folk Songs of the
  British Isles*, Vol. III (single)   BH
Chadwick, "A Ballad of Trees and the Master"   TP
Coates, "Bird Song at Eventide"   CHAP
Coates, "I Hear You Singing"   CHAP
Cox, "To a Hilltop"   GS
Elliot, "Spring's a Lovable Lady"   WB
Forsyth, "The Bellman"   TP
Gold, "Music When Soft Voices Die,"
  20th Century Art Songs   GS
Grieg, "With a Water Lily," *Pathways of Song*,
  Vol. III   WB
Hahn, "L'Heure Exquise" ("The Exquisite
  Hour"), *50 Art Songs from the Modern
  Repertoire*   GS
Hahn, "Were My Songs with Wings Provided"   GS
Hamblen, "This Is My Commandment"   CF
Handel, "Silent Worship"   JF
Handel, "Would You Gain the Tender
  Creature," *Imperial Edition*   BH
Head, "When I Think upon the Maidens"   BH
Ireland, "Sea Fever"   GAL/ECS
Keel, "Trade Winds"   BH
Klemm, "A Hundred Little Loves"   CF
McFayden, "Home"   SHM
Malotte, "The Twenty-Third Psalm"   GS

Martini, "The Joys Of Love" ("Plaisir
    D'Amour")   GS
Matthews, "The Lord Is My Shepherd"   FITZ
Mendelssohn, "On Wings of Song," *The*
    Young Singer (single)   CF
Munro, "My Lovely Celia," *The Young Singer*
    (single-BH)   CF
Niles, "Gambler, Don't Lose Your Place,"
    The Songs of John Jacob Niles   GS
Quilter, "Under the Greenwood Tree,"
    Five Shakespeare Songs, 2nd set   BH
Sacco, "Brother Will, Brother John,"
    20th Century Art Song   GS
Schubert, "Serenade"   GS
Secchi, "Love Me or Not"   BH
Sinding, "Sylvelin"   TP
Spross, "Let All My Life Be Music"   TP
Walton, "Under the Greenwood Tree"   OX
Willan, "O Perfect Love"   BEL

Grade C

Barber, "The Daisies"   GS
Beethoven, "I Love Thee," *Pathways of*
    Song, Vol. II   WB
Britten, "The Sally Gardens," *Folk Songs of*
    the British Isles, Vol. I   BH
Bury, "There Is a Lady"   CF
Darm, "Whenever My Mary Goes By"   BH
Densmore, "Roadways"   TP
Diack, "All in the April Evening"   BH
Dickson, "Thanks Be to God"   BH
Dougherty, "Rio Grande"   GS
Edwards, "Dedication"   GS
Franz, "Für Musik" ("For Music"), *Pathways of*
    Song, Vol. I   WB
Franz, "Gute Nacht" ("Good Night"),
    Pathways of Song, Vol. II   WB
Handel, "When First We Met"   OX
Haydn, "To Friendship"   WB
Hefferman, "The Watchman's Song,"
    Pathways of Song, Vol. II   WB
Hormer, "Sheep and Lambs"   GS
Legrenzi, "Che feiro costume"   TP
Lully, "Sombre Woods"   GS
Martini, "The Joys of Love"   GS
Mendelssohn, "On Wings of Song"   CF
Morgan, "Clorinda"   BH
Niles, "The Black Oak Tree"   CF
Purcell, "Passing By," *The Young Singer*
    (single-GS)   CF

Quilter, "The Ash Grove," *Arnold Book*
    of Old Songs   BH
Quilter, "Believe Me, If All Those
    Endearing Young Charms," *Arnold Book of*
    Old Songs   BH
Quilter, "Drink to Me Only with Thine Eyes,"
    Arnold Book of Old Songs   BH
Quilter, "Over the Mountains," *Arnold Book of*
    Old Songs   BH
Scott, "Think on Me"   GAL/ECS
Thompson, "My Master Hath a Garden"   ECS
Tosti, "Serenade"   GS
Willan, "O Perfect Love"   HWG
Wilson, "Mary of Allendale"   BH

Baritone

(Specify medium key when ordering)

Grade A

Barab, "A Maid Me Loved"   BH
Britten, "The Plough Boy"   BH
Britten, "The Ship of Rio"   OX
Butterworth, "When I Was One and Twenty,"
    11 Songs from A Shropshire Lad   GAL/ECS
Campbell-Tipton, "Hymn to the Night"   BEL
Carissimi, "Vittoria, Vittoria mio core,"
    24 Italian Songs and Arias   GS
Charles, "Incline Thine Ear"   GS
Charles, "My Lady Walks in Loveliness"   GS
Dello Joio, "There Is a Lady," *Contemporary*
    Songs in English (single)   CF
Dougherty, "Shenandoah"   GS
Dvořák, "Turn Thee to Me," *Biblical Songs*   AMP
Gore, "Entreat Me Not to Leave Thee"   CPH
Handel, "My father" (The Passion), *Anthology*
    of Sacred Songs   GS
Handel, "Silent Worship"   GS
Haydn, "Now Heaven in Fullest Glory"   GS
Head, "Money-O," *Imperial Edition: A Heritage*
    of 20th Century British Song (single)   BH
LaMontaine, "Stopping by Woods"   GAL/ECS
Landon, "O Lovely Night"   BH
Leoncavallo, "Mattinata," *Great Art Songs of*
    Three Centuries   GS
Malotte, "Song of the Open Road"   BRN/GS
Mendelssohn, "It Is Enough" (from *Elijah*)
    (single)   GS
Mendelssohn, "Lord, God of Abraham" (from
    Elijah) (single)   GS

Niles, "Gambler, Don't Lose Your Place,"
The Songs of John Jacob Niles   GS

Niles, "The Rovin' Gambler," *The Songs of
John Jacob Niles*   GS

Purcell, "An Evening Hymn"   HWG

Purcell, "I'll Sail upon the Dog Star"   INT

Quilter, "Blow, Blow Thou Winter Wind,"
Shakespeare Songs   BH

Quilter, "Come Away Death,"
Shakespeare Songs   BH

Schumann, "Die beiden Grenadiere"
(The Two Grenadiers)   GS

Schumann, "Widmung" ("Dedication")   GS

Scott, "Come, Ye Blessed"   GS

Scott, "The Old Road"   GS

Strauss, R., "Morgen"   GS

Tyson, "Sea Moods," *Songs by 22 Americans*   GS

Vaughan Williams, "Bright Is the Ring of
Words," *Songs of Travel* (single)   BH

Vaughan Williams, "The Roadside Fire,"
Songs of Travel (single)   BH

Vaughan Williams, "The Vagabond,"
Songs of Travel; *A Heritage of 20th Century
British Song*, Vol. I (single)   BH

Vaughan Williams, "Whither Must
I Wander," *Songs of Travel*; *A Heritage of
20th Century British Song*, Vol. I (single)   BH

Vaughan Williams, "Woodcutter's Song"   OX

Vaughan Williams, "Youth and Love,"
Songs of Travel; *A Heritage of 20th Century
British Song*, Vol. I   BH

Warlock, "My Own Country"   OX

Grade B

Beethoven, "In questa tomba"   GS

Bridge, "O That It Were So"   CHAP

Diers, "Stopping by Woods on a
Snowy Evening"   GAL/ECS

Dix, "The Trumpeter," *The Young Singer*   CF

Dougherty, "Blow Ye Winds"   GS

Dougherty, "Mobile Bay"   GS

Dvořák, "I Will Sing New Songs of Gladness,"
Biblical Songs   AMP

Dvořák, "Sing Ye a Joyful Song,"
Biblical Songs   AMP

Edmunds, "Praise We the Lord"   CF

Finzi, "Come Away, Come Away, Death,"
A Heritage of 20th Century British Song,
Vol. II   BH

Finzi, "Fear No More the Heat o' the Sun,"
A Heritage of 20th Century British Song,
Vol. II   BH

German, "Rolling Down to Rio"   BEL

Handel, "Rendi'l serene al ciglio," *Standard
Vocal Repertoire*, Book 2   CF

Head, "Acquaint Now Thyself with Him"   BH

Head, "Money"   BH

Head, "Thus Spake Jesus"   BH

Head, "When I Think upon the Maidens"   BH

Hely-Hutchinson, "Old Mother Hubbard"   CF

Homer, "Banjo Song"   GS

Hume, "Tobacco," *Imperial Edition*   BH

Keel, "Trade Winds"   BH

Leoni, "Tally Ho"   GS

Martini, "Plaisir d'amour"   GS

Morgan, "Clorinda"   BH

Munro, "My Lovely Celia"   BH

Niles, "The Gambler's Lament"   GS

Rorem, "Rain in Spring"   BH

Scott, "Lullaby"   GAL

Thiman, "The God of Love My
Shepherd Is"   HWG

Thiman, "Jesus, the Very Thought of Thee"   NOV

Vaughan Williams, "Whither Must I Wander"   GS

Warlock, "My Own Country"   OX

Grade C

American Folk, "Jesus, Jesus Rest Your Head"   CF

Clarke, "The Blind Ploughman"   CHAP

Dix, "The Trumpeter"   CF

Dougherty, "Across the Western Ocean,"
20th Century Art Songs (single)   GS

Dougherty, "Colorado Trail"   GS

Dvořák, "Hear My Prayer," *Biblical Songs*   AMP

Forsythe, "Tell Me Not a Lovely Lass"   HWG

German, "Rolling Down to Rio"   CF

Handel, "Verdant Meadows"   WB

Head, "The Lord's Prayer"   BH

Irish Folk, "Eileen Aroon," *Pathways
of Song*, Vol. II   WB

Morgan, "Clorinda"   BH

Niles, "The Gambler's Lament"   GS

Porter, "Music When Soft Voices Die"   TP

Purcell, "Next Winter Comes Slowly"   INT

Purcell, "Passing By," *The Young
Singer* (single-GS)   CF

Quilter, "Three Poor Mariners," *Arnold Book of
Old Songs*   BH

Quilter, "Over the Mountains," *Arnold Book of
Old Songs* (single)   BH

Row, arr., "Jesus, Jesus Rest Your Head,"
The Young Singer   CF

Taylor, "May Day Carol"   JF
Vaughan Williams, "Linden Lea"   BH

Bass
(Specify low key when ordering)

Grade A

Brahms, "O Tod wie bitter," *Four Serious Songs* GS
Butler, "The Lord Reigns," *The Solo
   Psalmist*   SMP/LOR
Debussy, "Beau soir"   BMC
Faure, "The Cradles"   WB
Handel, "Arm, Arm Ye Brave," *52 Sacred Songs* GS
Handel, "Si, tra i ceppi," *Great Art Songs of
   Three Centuries*   GS
Lully, "Bois epais"   BH
Moore, "Old Song," *Contemporary Songs in
   English* (single)   CF
Pergolesi, "Nina," *24 Italian Songs and Arias* GS
Schubert, "Whither"   GS
Schumann, "Die beiden Grenadiere"
   ("The Two Grenadiers"), *56 Songs You
   Like to Sing* (single)   GS
Sowerby, "The Lord Is My Shepherd"   BEL
Strauss, R., "Zueignung"   GS
Tchaikovsky, "The Pilgrim's Song,"
   The Young Singer (single-GS)   CF
Vaughan Williams, "The Roadside Fire,"
   *Songs of Travel; A Heritage of 20th Century
   British Song* (single)   BH
Vaughan Williams, "The Vagabond,"
   *Songs of Travel; A Heritage of 20th Century
   British Song* (single)   BH
Wolfe, "De Glory Road"   GS

Grade B

Andrews, "Sea Fever"   GS
Baksa, "When I Was One and Twenty"   BH
Banks, "Prayer of Saint Francis"   BEL
Bonds, "Joshua Fit the Battle of Jericho"   TP
Bowles, "Cabin," *20th Century Art Songs;
   Blue Mountain Ballads*   GS
Caccini, "Amarilli," *24 Italian Songs and Arias* GS
Carpenter, "May the Maiden"   TP
Chales, "The Sussex Sailor"   GS
Clarke, "The Blind Ploughman"   CHAP

Dougherty, "Blow Ye Winds"   GS
Dougherty, "Shenandoah"   GS
Duke, "Silver," *20th Century Art Songs* (single) GS
Dvořák, "Hear My Prayer," *Biblical Songs*   AMP
Handel, "Rendi'l sereno al ciglio," *Standard
   Vocal Repertoire*, Book 2   CF
Head, "Sweet Chance That Led My Steps"   BH
Ireland, "Sea Fever," *11 Songs by John
   Ireland*   GAL/ECS
Lehman, "Myself When Young"   BMC
Leoni, "Tally Ho"   GS
MacDermid, "In My Father's House Are
   Many Mansions"   FOR
McGill, "Duna"   BH
Thiman, "Thou Wilt Keep Him in Perfect
   Peace"   HWG
Ware, "This Day Is Mine"   BMC
Vaughan Williams, "The Roadside Fire"   BH

Grade C

Anon., "Down Among the Dead Men,"
   Imperial Edition   BH
Bach, "Come Sweet Death"   CF
Boatner, "I Want Jesus to Walk"   GAL/ECS
Britten, "The Sally Gardens," *Folk Songs of the
   British Isles*, Vol. I   BH
Brown, "Twenty-Third Psalm"   HWG
Copland, "I Bought Me a Cat," *Old American
   Songs*, Vol. I   BH
Copland, "The Dodger," *Old American Songs*,
   Vol. I   BH
Dodson, "Across the Western Ocean"   GS
Dougherty, "Blow Ye Winds"   GS
Dougherty, "Three Candles"   BMC
Edmunds, "Jesus, Jesus, Rest Your Head"   CF
Franz, "Widmung" ("Dedication")   GS
Hall, "Go to the Well"   BMC
Keel, "Trade Winds"   BH
Monteverdi, "Lasciatemi morire," *24 Italian
   Songs and Arias*   GS
Niles, "Black Is the Color"   GS
Pergolesi, "Nina"   TP
Quilter, "The Jolly Miller," *Arnold
   Book of Old Songs*   BH
Thiman, "The God of Love My
   Shepherd Is"   HWG
Wellesley, "Sing Me a Chantey"   SF/PLY

Vocal Solo Collections

Album of Sacred Songs (High, No. 1384; Low, No. 1385) — GS

Anthology of Italian Song, Books I and II — GS

Anthology of Modern French Songs (ed. Spicker). Vol. I, High; Vol. II, Low — GS

Anthology of Sacred Songs — GS

Arnold Book of Old Songs — BH

Art Songs for School and Studio (Glen and Sprouse). First Year, High and Low; Second Year, High and Low — TP

Bass Songs (ed. Mason) — TP

Best of Broadway, The, for Vocal Duet (Soprano and Alto and/or Soprano and Baritone) — HL

Biblical Songs (Dvořák) — GS

Brahms: Fifty Selected Songs. (Low, No. 1581; High, No. 1582) — GS

Broadway Repertoire: A Selection of Broadway's Best in Their Original Keys. Vol. I, Soprano; Vol. 2, Mezzo-Soprano; Vol. 3, Tenor; Vol. 4, Bass-Baritone. — CHAP

Collected Songs, Barber — GS

Contemporary American Art Songs — TP

Contemporary Art Songs — GS

Contemporary Songs in English — CF

Cycle of Three Mystical Songs, Rowley — BH

Eleven Songs by John Ireland — GAL/ECS

Eleven Songs from "A Shropshire Lad," Butterworth — GAL/ECS

Fifty Art Songs from the Modern Repertoire — GS

Fifty-Five Art Songs (Spaeth and Thompson) — SB

Fifty-Six Songs You Like to Sing — GS

Fifty-Two Sacred Songs — GS

Five Shakespeare Songs, 2nd Set, Quilter — BH

Folk Songs of the British Isles, Vols. I and III — BH

Foster, Stephen: Album of Songs, Twenty Favorites — GS

Four Songs, Berger — BRO

Four Traditional American Songs — ABI

Fourteen Songs on American Poetry — PET

Forty-Five Arias from Operas and Oratorios, Vol. II — INT

Franz, Robert: Vocal Album. (High, No. 1572; Low, No. 1573) — GS

French Art Songs — TP

French Art Songs for School and Studio (ed. Glenn and Taylor) — TP

Great Art Songs of Three Centuries — GS

Heritage of 20th Century British Song, Vols. I and II — BH

Imperial Edition — BH

Music for Sight Singing (Ottman) — PH

Old American Songs, Vols. I, II, and III — BH

One Hundred Hit Songs from Broadway's Greatest Musicals — CP

Operatic Anthology (ed. Spicker).
    Vol. I, Soprano; Vol. II, Mezzo-Soprano
    or Alto; Vol. III, Tenor; Vol. IV, Baritone;
    Vol. V, Bass   GS

Pathways of Song (LaForge and Earhart),
    Vol. I–IV, each for High and Low   WB

Schubert, Franz: Twenty-Four Favorite Songs.
    (High, No. 350; Low, No. 351)   GS

Sight Reading, See and Sing, Vols. I–III (Ehret) PRO

Singable Songs for Studio and Recital   TP

Solo Singer, The (Wilson). Vols. I and II,
    High and Low   CF

Songs of John Jacob Niles, The   GS

Songs of Travel   GS

Songs by Twenty-Two Americans   GS

Standard Repertoire, Book 2   CF

Standard Vocal Repertoire   WB

Three Shakespeare Songs, Quilter   BH

Twentieth Century Art Songs   GS

Twenty-Four Favorite Songs   GS

Twenty-Four Italian Songs and Arias   GS

Useful Teaching Songs (Lehmann).
    Vol. I, Soprano; Vol. II, Mezzo-Soprano;
    Vol. III, Alto; Vol. IV, Tenor;
    Vol. V, Bass   CHP

Young Singer, The   CF

Key to Publishers

AMP Associated Music Publishers, Inc.
    7101 West Field Ave., Pennsauken, New Jersey 08110 (GS)

BEL   Belwin/Mills Publishing Corp.
    6744 N.E. 4th Ave., Miami, Florida 33138 (CP)

BH   Boosey & Hawkes, Inc.
    Lawson Blvd., P.O. Box 130, Oceanside, New York 11572

BMC   Boston Music Co.
    116 Boylston St., Boston, Massachusetts 02116

BR/ABI Basil Ramsey/Alexander Broude, Inc.
    225 West 57th St., New York, New York 10019

BRN   Bourne Music Co.
    437 Fifth Ave., New York, New York 10016

BRO   Broude Brothers, Inc.
    56 West 45th St., New York, New York 10036

CF   Carl Fischer, Inc.
    62 Cooper Sq., New York, New York 10003

CHAP Chappell and Co., Inc.
    8112 West Blue Mound Rd., Milwaukee, Wisconsin 53123 (HL)

COL   Franco Colombo Publications
    6744 N.E. 4th Ave., Miami, Florida 33138 (BEL)

CP   Columbia Pictures
    6744 N.E. 4th Ave., Miami, Florida 33138

EBM   Edward B. Marks Music Corp.
    8112 West Blue Mound Rd., Milwaukee, Wisconsin 63213 (HL)

ECS   E.C. Schirmer Music Co.
    112 South St., Boston, Massachusetts 02111

FITZ   Fitzsimmons Music Publishers
    615 North LaSalle, Chicago, Illinois 60610

GAL   Galaxy Music Corp.
    112 South St., Boston, Massachusetts 02111 (ECS)

GS   G. Schirmer Inc.
    7101 West Field Ave., Pennsauken, New Jersey 08110

HL   Hal Leonard Publishing Corp.
    8112 West Blue Mound Rd., Milwaukee, Wisconson 53213

HWG   H. W. Gray Co., Inc.
    6744 N.E. 4th Ave., Miami, Florida 33138 (BEL)

INT   International Music Corp.
    545 Fifth Ave., New York, New York 10017

JEN   Jenson Publications, Inc.
    P.O. Box 248, 2880 South 171st St., New Berlin, Wisconsin 53151

JF   J. Fischer & Bros.
    6744 N.E. 4th Ave., Miami, Florida 33138 (BEL)

LOR   Lorenz Industries
    501 East Third St., Dayton, Ohio 45401

MM   Mercury Music Corp.
    Presser Place, Bryn Mawr, Pennsylvania 19010 (TP)

NOV   Novello and Company, Ltd.
    Presser Place, Bryn Mawr, Pennsylvania 19010 (TP)

OX   Oxford University Press
    1600 Pollitt Pl., Fairlawn, New Jersey 07410

PET   C. F. Peters Corp.
    373 Park Ave. South, New York, New York 10016

PH   Prentice-Hall
    Englewood Cliffs, New Jersey 07632

PLY   Plymouth Music Co., Inc.
         170 Northeast 33rd St., Ft. Lauderdale, Florida 33334

PRO   Pro Art Publications
         6744 N.E. 4th Ave., Miami, Florida 33138 (BEL)

SF   Sam Fox Publishing Co.
         170 North 33rd St., Ft. Lauderdale, Florida 33334 (PLY)

SHM   Schmitt, Hall, and McCreary Co.
         6744 N.E. 4th Ave., Miami, Florida 33138 (BEL)

SMP   Southern Music Publishing Co.
         1740 Broadway, New York, New York 10019

SU   Summy-Birchard Co.
         P.O. Box CN 27, Princeton, New Jersey 08540

TP   Theodore Presser Co.
         Presser Place, Bryn Mawr, Pennsylvania 19010

WB   Warner Brothers Publications, Inc.
         P.O. Box 248, 2880 South 171st St., New Berlin, Wisconsin 53151 (JEN)

WEIN   Weintraub Music Co.
         P.O. Box 152, Chester, New York 10918

WIL   Willis Music Co.
         7380 Industrial Road, Florence, Kentucky 41042